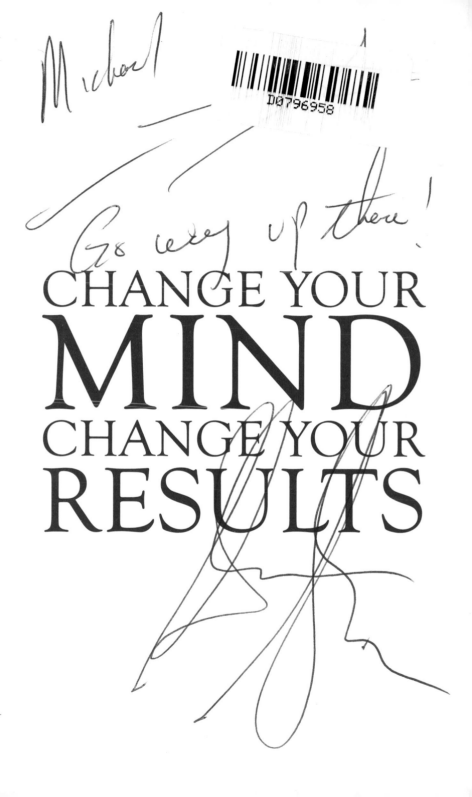

CHANGE YOUR
MIND
CHANGE YOUR
RESULTS

Quantity discounts are available on bulk orders.
Contact info@TAGPublishers.com for more information.

TAG Publishing, LLC
2618 S. Lipscomb
Amarillo, TX 79109
www.TAGPublishers.com
Office (806) 373-0114
Fax (806) 373-4004
info@TAGPublishers.com

ISBN: 978-1-59930-312-3

First Edition

CHANGE YOUR MIND CHANGE YOUR RESULTS

#1 Proven Success Strategies

SHAWN SHEWCHUK

ABOUT THE AUTHOR

Shawn Shewchuk is widely regarded as a leader in the area of achievement and performance, and has skyrocketed to being one of the most sought after speakers, coaches and wealth building authorities in the country. Through his coaching, speaking, bestselling and ground-breaking system, The Power of A™ – Strategic Accountability he has transformed the results of countless individuals and numerous organization around the world.

Shawn Shewchuk is the direct link to the achievement of your objectives. The outcomes experienced by those he has worked with have been so remarkable that he has been called the Big Results Authority.™ His company Change Your Results! is headquartered in Western Canada but operates globally. Visit **www.changeyourresults.com**

This book is dedicated to:

My late father, for the powerful lessons in life, business, ethics and relentless persistence. Without these fundamental cornerstones, I would not be where I am today.

My miracle son, who inspires me daily to reach for the stars.

Someone very special who recently left this world. It was a chance meeting with this individual, that so impacted me, I decided to share my experience with you.

ACKNOWLEDGEMENTS

I would like to acknowledge and thank the entire publishing team for their tireless work and phenomenal effort in the preparation of this book. I am truly grateful that they tolerated my incessant emails and telephone calls.

Thank you to my support team for putting up with the many hours of writing, re-writing and requested assistance. Your support and inspiration are deeply appreciated. In addition, I would like to express my heartfelt gratitude to my immense circle of amazing and wonderful family, friends, clients and colleagues, for their support and belief in me. Some of whom made it into the book anonymously.

An enormous thank you to Jessica Hall for the countless hours assisting me in the preparation of the manuscript.

Finally, words cannot describe how truly grateful I am to Bob Proctor for his friendship and tremendous support. Thank you Bob for inspiring me to share this message with the world, and for writing the foreword to this book.

CONTENTS

FOREWORD

For over 40 years I've taught the principles that help people get what they want from their business and personal lives and in all that time I've learned one great truth. Success doesn't just happen; you choose that success by the decisions you make each and every day. Shawn Shewchuk is at the forefront of those professionals who are helping others move forward and succeed with proven strategies for success.

No matter where you start in life, you can overcome any challenge and succeed. Shawn is an excellent example of this type of courage having experienced it in his own life. Though born into an economically disadvantaged situation, Shawn chose to reject the idea that he had to be satisfied with that life and made the decision to change. That decision was all it took to start him down the path to prosperity.

Shawn Shewchuk is now a successful business owner and entrepreneur who shares his story and principles for success with others. A highly sought after mentor, consultant, and speaker, Shawn can help guide you through the steps to improve your life by expanding what you believe is possible. Within these pages, you will learn how to break free from old ideas that are holding you back. You will also understand that you have the ability to create your own economy and prosper no matter what is going on in the world at large.

Change Your Mind, Change Your Results will be a resource you can refer to repeatedly to help you discover and achieve what you really want in life. Rarely are those things we perceive to be problems in our daily lives really problems at all. We have just convinced ourselves that no solutions exist. This book will allow you to explore the reasons behind your thoughts and actions which will give you the awareness you need to change your results.

You already hold the keys to your success within you, but if no one ever shows you how to recognize the seeds of your potential, you won't achieve all that is possible. Even if you are convinced that you cannot break free from your current situation, this book will change your mind. Anyone can offer you steps for change, but Shawn also offers you hope. Once you understand that real change comes from within, you will see the new abundant life that awaits and is there for you if you but choose to accept it.

Bob Proctor,
International Speaker,
Author of *You Were Born Rich*

INTRODUCTION

Don't wait. The time will never be just right.
Napoleon Hill

A wise man once gave me some wonderful advice, he said: "Shawn, if you live your life in the past, your past will become your future." That man is no longer with us, but his advice was timely and applicable. I have to admit, those words irritated me. My life was just fine, or so I thought. There's no way he can know anything about me or my business, and I was convinced I knew the path to my success.

It wasn't until a couple of years later that these words came back and hit me across the face with the force of a brick. I had been trying my best, but it seemed as if everything in my life went into a continuing downward spiral. In fact, the harder I tried, the worse things became. There is an old saying that if you keep trying to do things the same way and keep getting the same results, you are heading for a life of insanity. Indeed, I had been creating my future all along, and it was simply a replay of my past. I realized that something had to change, if I was ever going to have the life I truly wanted.

I am confident that every person, at some point in their life has encountered challenges that perhaps at the time, may have seemed insurmountable. The reality is, as you may have already figured out, that most of the daily challenges that we are faced with in our lives, businesses, careers or relationships are typically simple to conquer. The keys are perspective and accountability!

You see, when I was young I didn't have many examples of very successful people. I was born into a family that although loving, had very little money and even less of the finer things that a great many of us take for granted. My father worked extremely hard to provide for his family, but at times we still struggled financially. By the time I was in my teens, my father had been able to put us on the path of a somewhat comfortable lifestyle, although we certainly never reached 'wealthy' status. Money was tight no matter what stage of the economic continuum we found ourselves in. Out of their belief of necessity, my parents were frugal and keenly aware of what it was like to go without even the basic essentials.

As a result of a very strict upbringing and negatively reinforced motivation, my self-confidence was low and this doubt about my abilities discouraged me from even attempting anything, let alone finishing it. I had good parents who loved me deeply, but I was raised as they were raised, not knowing there was a better way. It took some time but I was eventually able to overcome my lack of confidence, occasionally it continued to adversely affect my performance.

Most of the decisions that we make in our lives are based on unsolicited gifts from our parents, educators and religious exposure. Although we may initially deny it, most of the decisions that we make as adults, are not our own. This is the reason that we see children following in the steps of their parents, whether they want to or not.

I had disappointing experiences with many jobs when I was young, even though I tried as hard as I could. As I look back, I can see these struggles and challenges were because I tried so hard to force things to happen, and I was always focused on what I didn't want to happen. This also carried over into my personal life. In my early twenties, I met my first wife and we quickly married. During this period, I was far too absorbed with work, leaving little, if any, time for anything or anyone else.

I was so busy building what I *thought* was a good living that it came at the exclusion of everything else, the things that should have been important. I neglected everything except work, and my life became more unbalanced with each month that passed. I had been taught what many others are taught when they are young; that in order to get ahead you must work hard. My father and grandfather were firm believers that if you were not getting the results you wanted, you had to simply work harder. I believed this and by my mid to late twenties, I was a workaholic and I knew it. Please understand, that I did make my own decisions but as always, our decisions are typically based on the examples we have seen and the beliefs that are instilled in us.

This same mindset carried over to my finances as well. I accumulated debt to build this life that I thought I was supposed to have, but the more I focused on paying off that debt, the more it seemed to accumulate. Sure, I was *earning* great money, but I was also *spending* more than I was *making*. It was a vicious cycle from which I felt I could not escape and I couldn't quite figure out how other people seemed to get by. So I worked even harder. I invested in real estate and other business ventures, which were actually doing quite well, but I had already been on the wrong track for enough years that it finally caught up with me.

Within three months, I found myself jobless, bankrupt, and in divorce court. The house of cards I had built with my job, investments and even my marriage crumbled, completely disintegrating as if by a sudden earthquake. My credit was destroyed and I was homeless! This was definitely not the way things were supposed to go.

Where I ended up, has a great deal to do with what I was focused on. You see, I should have been focused on what I wanted and not on what I didn't want.

I have heard it said that many a wealthy person started their journey in the heart of financial disaster, and that is exactly where I was – a disaster. I had worked myself into the ground and not only did I have nothing to show for it, I was worse off than I ever imagined myself being. I vowed that I would never allow this situation to occur in my life again and that I'd do anything to prevent it. I am pleased to report that I have lived up to that pledge, but it has been a journey of challenges and persisting when things got tough.

Once I really grasped the idea that I could create my own life starting right now, no matter what had happened in the past, I made real strides in my life. I didn't sit around and keep doing the same things I'd always done and beat my head against the proverbial wall. I'd already been there, done that, and it was a disaster! I could see that there were people out there that knew the secret to true success, and I committed to educating myself and achieving that same success.

No matter what it is you truly want in life, you can achieve it! Every one of us has been given the gift of infinite potential and I know you may not really believe that right now. You may be exactly where I was back then - head down, slogging through the day just hoping against hope that something will come along and save you. I'm here to tell you that change can happen in an instant or in a day, or it can take the rest of your life – it's up to you and it's your choice. No one is going to save you unless you commit to saving yourself, just as I did.

Think about it for a second, you have nothing to lose and a life to gain!

I come from a business and management consulting background, and over the years my career has naturally progressed into the realm of coaching, although I'm not sure that coaching is the right word. It's through this medium that I'm able to explain the infinite possibilities that are afforded to each person. Having said that, it truly is about more than what you can achieve, it's about your life, your business or career, and your relationships. It's about having the money that you want and need, it's about building and/or managing a profitable business, or building the career of your dreams. It's also about the relationships that you build in your life, business or career.

This is a message that needs to get out, but there is only one of me, so I penned this book to effectively communicate some core concepts that have proven highly successful in helping people achieve greater results in all aspects of their lives. This allows you to access these ideas and start implementing them right away. This is just a very small preview of what you will be learning within the pages of this book. Now you will know what to expect and what kind of benefits you will receive.

Whenever I start working with a client or student we usually have to spend some time on the past. All of us are shaped by our experiences and what we have learned. But often these beliefs and ideas don't benefit us now, and can even stand in the way of our success. You have to completely grasp that your past does not equal your future – and then let it go. Remaining stuck in the past is a sure way to make sure that you never fully arrive at the future you want. You must get past what is holding you back before you can take the first steps to building your new and well balanced life.

Few people ever realize how much useless rhetoric we allow into our minds each day. Other individuals, and the media, are constantly bombarding us with negative images, gossip, tales of woe and every kind of chatter that convinces many of us that trying for a better life is hopeless. For example, have you ever told someone that you were going to start your own business? I'm sure that even as the words left your mouth; someone was discouraging you with business failure statistics and stories of disaster encountered by other business owners they've heard about. For these reasons, it is important to protect your mind from this negativity, and understand that you have the power to find opportunities that may lie hidden beneath the rhetoric. It's a matter of developing the mental fortitude to evaluate all the facts and then summon the courage to go your own way. If everyone else was right, they would all be wealthy and living their dream. In reality, how many people do you know that are actually living that dream? Ten? Three? One? None? Why are you listening to those who have no clue how to achieve success?

The title of this book is: *Change Your Mind, Change Your Results.* It's also the name of the signature chapter of the book and the inspiration behind the name of my company, Change Your Results! www.changeyourresults.com. It showcases my extremely simple, yet effective, method to help you achieve the goals that really matter in your life. The basis of this change is to explore and understand how our minds work, and why we behave the way we do. In order to really change, you have to first know how to effect change, and we talk about this in-depth in chapter four, so you have a foundation of understanding before you take action.

We already touched on the fact that for the first portion of my life I lacked self-confidence. It's been my experience that even the most confident person will have the occasional 'crisis of faith' in themselves and may question what they are really capable of achieving. Without the necessary confidence in your ability to overcome and achieve great things, you will never approach your desires with the required commitment to endure the struggle associated with the journey. Aside from a deficit in self-confidence, another common source of indecision that people experience is that they don't know what they want in the first place. I will give you the tools to really explore what you want and understand that it is different for every person.

From there we will launch into the process of creating a plan to attain your goals, and then implement that plan to ensure your results. This means knowing how to monitor your own progress and understand that instead of making mistakes, you are getting feedback as you travel along, that will help you get to where you want to be. Often we criticize ourselves and intentionally beat up our own sense of self-worth over relatively minor errors in judgment. I will help you let go of that self-criticism and move forward using the knowledge gained in times of challenge.

You will encounter obstacles any time you want to implement change. It is how you face these trying times that defines who you want to be as a person, and shows you the kind of person you can strive to be. The road will not be easy, but that will make the attainment of your goal all the more satisfying. If it were easy, everyone would have what they want, and the fact that so few do, is proof that you must work for it and be persistent.

There is no better time to start than right now. You can choose the path of least resistance that leads to dissatisfaction and disappointment, or you can choose the road less traveled, to great heights. It's your choice and only you can make the decision.

I believe that you were born with a purpose, and I also believe that you were given the corresponding talent and passion to live, and fulfill that purpose. It's time to utilize your gifts and create the change that you long for in your life. Time is a thief and every moment that passes is time lost from the life you really want. Go after your dream! It was always intended that you live a prosperous and abundant life, and the only thing stopping you from having that life right now is you. If you think otherwise, then you may not be ready to accept what is rightfully yours. But if you believe, as I do, that you truly deserve the best life possible, then you will be amazed at what you can accomplish. Are you ready to make a decision to change your results? Then let's get started.

CHAPTER 1

COMPLETE PARALYSIS

Courage is going from failure to failure without losing enthusiasm.
Winston Churchill

Many of us like to sit around and think about the glory days. Transporting ourselves back in time, we think about all the wonderful things that happened in the past. Unfortunately, we also like to incessantly beat ourselves up over our past mistakes and transgressions as well. How often have you thought your life would be better if you had taken this job rather than that one, or if you'd held your tongue instead of speaking your mind, or if you'd jumped at a particular opportunity instead of letting it walk right past you? This type of thought process often overrides the positive emotions that we may associate with the past. We repeatedly focus on and live out the troubles and problems that we have faced, and the circumstances that may have shaped our current unpleasant or unsatisfactory reality.

It goes without saying that this is an incredibly destructive way of thinking, yet we all do it at one time or another. The problem with living in the past is that it paralyzes us, denying us access to the unending beauty of what lies ahead. There are actually two key destructive elements in play here.

The first is that we are limiting ourselves based on prior circumstances. We think that if we can't even do that right, how could we aspire to something grander? People become so identified with the past that they inevitably let it define their future, and refuse to see that there is more. The second part of the equation is that people tend to focus so intently on the negative aspects in their lives that they attract more of it into their world.

We all know people who constantly chatter about how bad things are; their job, their home life, their money situation – everything seems to be a disaster. And it is. As they focus on all the bad, more bad comes to them, and then as they focus on the new bad circumstances, even more negativity is drawn into their lives. This is a classic case of the Law of Attraction at work. This law states that whatever you concentrate on and believe, whether it is bad or good, you will attract more of, into your life. Whether you believe in the Law of Attraction or you utilize the Law of Attraction, it is always working. It's always bringing you what you ask of it.

Of course this begs the question, if you can choose what you are bringing into your life, why on earth would you choose the bad? Let's try this a different way; if you tell me that you don't believe in the Law of Attraction then think about this for a moment - look at successful people throughout history, right up to today, perhaps you know someone that fits this description. What do they all have in common? We aren't going to answer this question right now, but as you read through this book the answer will become apparent to you. When this answer becomes apparent to you, it may shock you and you may wonder, as I did, why you hadn't thought of it before.

It is important to believe that whatever happened in your past is of no consequence to you today. I don't mean you have to say it, you must absolutely believe this to be true.

What has transpired in the past is irrelevant to your future achievements. You cannot change what happened in the past, but you can change what happens in 10 minutes, tomorrow, next month or 10 years from now. You must retrain your mind to concentrate on the things that you can change, and let go of the things over which you no longer have control. Release all those regrets and the "coulda, woulda, shoulda" thoughts. They can't help you and in fact will drag you down. Let them go and embrace your future with new hope and clarity. You have the power within you to make changes in your life today that will help shape your reality, no matter what you desire that reality to be.

Other than the educational value, your successes or failures of the past are totally irrelevant; whether you want to start a new business, become a better leader in your current position, make a certain amount of money or create and develop better and stronger relationships. Remember this, what got you to where you are isn't going to take you where you want to go.

As I described in the introduction, I have seen a few hardships in my life. It took me a number of years to be able to get out of my destructive mindset. Though it didn't happen overnight, it didn't take as long as I would have guessed in the beginning. The change started incrementally as I made small redirections in the way I thought, talked and acted.

Eventually, the frequency with which things were changing started to increase. I attracted into my life the things that I wanted, the things that I truly desired. These results confirmed that I was on the right path and gave me the encouragement to keep going. In a relatively short period of time, I met a very special woman, built a great home, bought a new car and as a result of achieving my goals became a much happier person.

This gradual compounding of occurrences eventually became a tidal wave of success. I made a quantum leap into the life that I created for myself, and it was far different and better than anything I dreamed of previously.

For all practical purposes, if the past was any indication of the future, I wouldn't have been able to lead the life I am currently leading. I would have been consigned to a life of the struggling masses, trying to get ahead and deal with my apathy and misery. All it took was that one spark of belief that I could change, and that it was really possible to go a different direction. I believed and then acted accordingly. Oh, I still worked very hard, but there was a new passion for what I was creating.

I felt in control and the turning point was reached when I realized that my past was not necessarily representative of my future. The only way my life would continue the way it had been, was if I believed it was true and failed to execute any changes. I realized of course that I could change. Don't get me wrong, it didn't come easy. I have worked hard; I have made sacrifices.

You too, will have to work hard and make difficult choices along the way, but the road to the life you truly desire starts with realizing that you do not have to remain stuck in the past.

You may have heard people talk about paradigms, but what does that really mean? Paradigms are nothing more than a group of habits—both good and bad. Interestingly, most of the habits we employ aren't even our own. If you stop and think about it, you will realize that most of us have allowed our parents, grandparents, religious leaders, educators and others to define what we believe and how we perceive life.

From a very early age, we have based our daily decisions and opinions on the information fed to us by others. These beliefs and values have become habits, and we have operated in this manner for so long that many of us are not even aware of the origin of our beliefs.

Unfortunately, this applies not only to our knowledge base, but also to how we view our capabilities. Here's an example: "Oh, pay no mind to little Johnny. He's just a dreamer." Sound familiar? If you haven't been told that directly, it is likely that you have at least heard it said to someone else. Beliefs like "He's a dreamer" become entrenched within every fiber of our being and make up who we believe ourselves to be. We are all dreamers, but too often we are told to let go of childish dreams and pursue something real. We are told to be practical. Our aspirations are stifled, written off as a lack of attention to what our teacher, or someone else, is telling us is important. You may have been sitting in class when the teacher said, "Hey! Snap out of it! Do your assignments. Stop dreaming! Why don't you watch what the other kids are doing? Why don't you just follow along?" This insistence on conformity and following someone else soon becomes a habit and is ingrained in the way we approach all aspects of our lives.

We are taught to be conformists from a young age, and it continues to permeate our lives when we become adults. It carries over. Nobody wants to stand out from the crowd for fear that they will be ostracized, and all it started in childhood.

The sad part is that these ideas we believed as a child, are what we base adult life-altering decisions on. Whether it's our lives, our business, our careers, no matter what it is, we tend to approach things in the way we are accustomed to and comfortable with.

It is important to understand that whether we are talking about ourselves with respect to our daily lives, or as employees or business owners, we must change and we must adapt. Change happens constantly and the world around us is in perpetual motion – yet we behave as if nothing ever changes, which is contrary to the evidence we see each day. It has been proven time and again that if we are stagnant, we're going to fail. As Bob Proctor, international personal development expert, likes to say: "Create or Disintegrate." We are either moving forward or we are going backward. In order to tap into that source of power within, you must strive to continually grow. It is not enough to just maintain the status quo or even to take one tiny step, it must be ongoing. Growth is critical to fulfillment in business, career, life and relationships.

So often we limit ourselves not only in what we have accomplished to date, but what we can achieve in the future. We relegate ourselves to a place today that is no better than where we were in the past. People experience recurring thoughts such as: "I come from a poor family so there is no way I could ever find myself among the likes of the Rockefellers." I have actually had people tell me such things, though they have absolutely no basis in fact.

I also hear things such as: "I grew up on a farm. What do I know about running a corporation?" "My parents never went to college, so I'll be lucky if I can just make it out of high school. I'm not cut out for college." You can also translate these statements into ones that apply to any other aspect of your personal or professional life.

These are of course incredibly debilitating points of view which have nothing to do with your potential or objectives. Where you came from, or what happened in the past, has no bearing on what you are capable of today or tomorrow. We are caught in the trap of allowing the past, the history of our lives, to dictate and influence where we go in the future. You must break free from this way of thinking in order to embrace your full potential.

It is true that what we experience today is a direct result of our thoughts from the past. That doesn't mean that today's results determine tomorrow's. What we *think* today, will definitely have an impact on our future. There is a direct correlation between the goals we set today and what happens tomorrow. Again, what you thought yesterday resulted in where you are today. What you think today is going to effect tomorrow, next week, next month, next year, ten years and beyond. If we can get out of the mindset of concentrating so heavily on what happened in the past, on where we come from or even where we are currently, we can achieve whatever we desire. It's been said that whether they'll admit it or not, every person is exactly where he or she wants to be, because if they wanted to be elsewhere they would do something about it. I assure you that statement is 100% accurate.

You don't have to have it all figured out, and you don't have to currently possess all of the resources that you believe are necessary for future success. In truth, you already have all you need right now, no matter where you begin your journey. Most successful people were not born with a silver spoon in their mouths. This is not to say that there are not exceptions, there certainly are, but most people of high stature followed a simple formula: they set goals and worked toward them. Look at the vast majority of people today who are at the top of their field: Actors, actresses, business people, executives, and entrepreneurs. Most of these people, some with education, most without, didn't come from money. Most of them simply had a goal and turned it into reality, regardless of their circumstances. There is one aspect of their successes that they all had in common, and that is accountability.

Bill Gates is a college dropout; yet he imagined what could be, to the point that his systems and ideas affect almost every minute of our day. His inventions and innovations effect how we communicate, how much knowledge we have access to, and what we can accomplish from nearly any place on the planet. Though it may seem like it's been a long time for these to evolve, in reality, it's been a short forty years from idea to worldwide application and reliance. He had a vision as a very young, very green, inexperienced kid. Yet, he literally changed the world we live in over a few short decades, because he refused to listen when others told him he couldn't achieve.

One of the problems many of us run into is that we not only judge ourselves based on our past, but we don't give people who are successful enough credit. We tend to say, "Oh, how lucky that person is. If only I could have what they have been given." The truth is that they are not lucky, and more often than not, they have not been given a thing. They have worked for everything they have acquired. Take a professional athlete for example: Do you have any idea how hard Wayne Gretzky worked on his game? To watch "The Great One" move around the ice during the height of his career was like watching an artist. Sure, he had natural talent and ability to become arguably the most dominant athlete in his sport ever, takes a heck of a lot of hard work. He had passion for the game; he truly loved to play.

Don't make the mistake of thinking that you can just decide on a goal and if it is meant to be, it will happen. Sports don't work that way, and neither does life, or business for that matter. You have to be excited and passionate about your goal, and relentlessly pursue it. You can't let anyone deter you or knock you off track. How do you think people would react to a young kid who tells them, "I'm going to be the greatest hockey goal scorer and play-maker of all time." There would naturally be doubt, but you can't let it affect you. No matter what your goal is, make up your mind and do it, regardless of who you are or where you have been. Remember, all you have to know is where you are going, it's also a really good idea to have someone to help you along the way.

As Napoleon Hill said in his classic work, *Think and Grow Rich*, you must have a near obsession and a burning desire to achieve your goal. In studying over 500 of the most successful and influential people of his time, Hill found a common thread. These people didn't worry about nine to five; they weren't operating on bankers' hours. They did what was necessary and did not let others dictate what was possible. Too many people allow others to put a stop to their journey, before they even take a single step. They become frustrated and deterred when they hear things like, "You have no idea how to run a business. What makes you so special? Why can't you just be satisfied with what you have?"

These questions can be especially damaging when the sentiment comes from those closest to us. We allow the detractors in our family, and within our group of friends, to squelch our dreams. I realize this may be a sensitive topic, but being inundated by such comments may be an indication that we should take a closer look at those people who are a negative influence on us. We may need to limit our time with them. The people you spend time with will directly influence your results in your life. If you are around a continuously negative person, someone who is always feeling down, someone who is always complaining and gossiping about other people, that will unquestionably impact your life if you allow it.

I have a relative who has a perpetually sour disposition. I love this person dearly, but I must limit the amount of time I spend with this person because of the constant negative energy. "Did you hear what happened? I can't believe so-and-so did that, and he said this. I can't believe he's such a sorry so and so." This person's whole life centers around finding the most negative aspect of any situation. Even more interesting is the fact that this person seems to take a type of warped pride in the fact that they are so harsh and critical. This relative has stated to me, "I'm cranky. I'm bitter. I'm old and I have no money in the bank; I have debt; I can't retire, and I'm tired of working." Can you understand how destructive it can be to constantly spend time around this person? You must be careful with whom you associate, friends and family included.

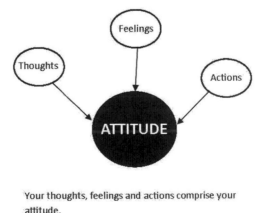

Your thoughts, feelings and actions comprise your attitude.

If you are associating with somebody in your life who is negative and constantly complaining, you will inadvertently start to emulate those same ideals. This in turn influences your attitude. Attitude is made up of your thoughts, feelings and actions and these can be influenced by both negative and positive people. Our attitude controls everything in our lives. So if we have a negative attitude, the outcome that we get in our lives is going to reflect negative results. It is like a continuous cycle of negativity that robs you of your potential. This is a major problem with many people. They have become so focused on what others say, or they allow others to dictate what goes into their minds, to the point that they are defeated before they take the first step. They lose the will to try for something better and as they limit themselves, they also close the door on life's potential abundance.

We all have a tendency to limit ourselves in this way on occasion. We doubt ourselves. We find a way to allow our past or current circumstances to convince us that maybe we can't achieve. We find innumerable reasons why we can't do something and put off taking action as long as possible. Age is one of these perpetual excuses we use for not doing what we say we want to do. It goes something like this: "I'm only twenty years old. What can I do, I'm too young?" or "I'm sixty years old. I can't do that, I'm too old!"

I had a woman come up to me in one of my seminars and say, "You know, Shawn, I'm seventy-eight years old. I can't change." I can't tell you how sad it makes me to hear people dismiss themselves. The most egregious aspect of that statement is that she is flat out wrong. I don't care how old you are. You can always make changes to improve your life. Start from where you are right now. There is no reason why you cannot achieve your dreams. Just because they may seem distant, or improbable due to where you come from, or where you are right now, that is no reason not to go for it.

I met Jack a few years back on vacation in the Caribbean. We were chatting with some transplanted locals in a restaurant about what it was like to retire to the area, and Jack was sitting at a table next to us. He had white hair, but sported a great tan and obviously loved living in the Caribbean. I honestly believed him to be in his fifties as he was energetic and laughed with us. After we talked a while, he shared that he'd almost missed out on living this life. He'd lived in the Washington, D.C. area for most of his life and worked in high level government positions. He lead an expected life, marrying his college sweetheart, having three children and a well planned career. Two years before he had thought they would retire, his wife died of cancer after only a short illness. He said he wandered around the house for months alone, and it was as if he could feel himself aging and wasting away.

One day when he was cleaning out a closet he ran across some brochures for some retirement communities in the Caribbean. You see, he and his wife had researched retiring to the Caribbean before her passing. He sat at the kitchen table with them and knew he had a choice to make. He could stay where he was, and continue to live his 'expected' life slowly dying a little each day, or he could pack his bags and live the life they had dreamed of. Needless to say he packed his bags and never looked back! It was a perfect example of someone who actively chose change and benefited immensely from it. By the way, when I met him, Jack had just turned 73!

It is entirely possible that you can make small changes, and focus your efforts on areas that will eventually lead to your own quantum leap, to the life you desire. The point of this book is to inspire as many of you as I can to explore and expand the awareness of your potential. Not only that, but help you understand that with a little extra effort, tenacity and of course accountability to your coach, you will get better results. It doesn't take much.

If you devote even a small amount of time to making changes, you will be surprised at the positive progress you will make. It matters not what your specific goals are, as everyone's will be different. You just have to be able to break from the past, replace your bad habits, and replace your old paradigms. You may be thinking: "Can I really change? Can I break the habits that I have held my whole life?" Of course you can. People do it all the time. As a coach, I see them do it every day.

Studies show that it takes a human being on average about three weeks to form a new habit. Make the effort to make slight adjustments to your behavior that will have a lasting impact. If money is your goal, and you put in that extra hour today to create more income, you're going to make an extra dollar or two tomorrow. If you put in two extra hours, you will get twice as much and it grows from there.

Here is a great method of ensuring positive change in your life, the lives of your family, your business or career. But before I tell you how to effectively change your paradigms quickly, you must be ready for change. If you are ready, this will work for you. Here we go.

Pick two habits that you want to change, these could be anything: smoking, unhealthy eating, your quick temper. Now, what is the polar opposite of those two habits? Now, focus on the polar opposite of your habits for 30 days. You may slip up, and that is ok. You must then re-start your 30 day trial. Every time you slip up, you have to re-start your 30 day trial.

What we're talking about is going from where you are today to where you want to be, in a relatively short period of time. I did this myself when I went from making $15,000 a year to making six figures. It didn't happen overnight, but with some hard work and commitment, it didn't take that long either. You can expand on these principles and reach the specific goals that you outline for yourself. This is not a farce or some unproven theory. I have done it myself and I help others do it consistently. This book will show you how to get there. The first rule bears repeating: You cannot let your past or current circumstances define your future.

While working for me, a young man who was 26 years old, said, "Shawn, I need your help." "What is it?" I asked. "I need to understand how this works. Can you help?"

This was one of my employees. I never told him he needed to do this, but here we have a twenty-six year old person who is taking the first step toward a better life. I can't claim to fully understand the specifics of your life situation, or your past, but you know what? It doesn't matter; because I know that no matter who you are or where you come from, you can achieve whatever you want in your life. You can do it. If you have an education great, if not, so what, neither did Bill Gates. It doesn't matter who your parents were, what they did or didn't do, what nationality or religion you are— ANYBODY can do this.

The problem is that we get so focused on money in the short term that we lose sight of the bigger picture. "I have a mortgage today; I have a car payment tomorrow; I have a credit card payment the following day." We must zero-in on what we actually want to achieve in the larger sense, not on the daily concerns that compete for our attention. If we focus on debt, we will, of course, attract yet more debt into our lives. If you are planning great things for your life, and all you do is focus on all the things that went wrong, then you will continue to be bogged down with more negative results. You must look forward, focus on your goal and release the past.

Decide on your passion and then a plan of action that works for you, but don't just blindly follow the pack. People often call me and complain about their current state and wonder what to do. "I've been working in multilevel marketing for about three years, and I only have two people in my downline, but I am working hard at it every day." Well, perhaps you need to reconsider your goals and reevaluate where you are going. Maybe that is not the right business venture for you and not really where your talent and passion lies. Perhaps you need to look at something else. This is by no means a deterrent to those in multilevel marketing, which can be as successful as any other business endeavor. My point is that you need to be able to wake up in the morning and enjoy what you are doing. At a minimum, you need to relish the thought of where you are going that day. It is a choice you must make for yourself and it starts by asking, "What gets me out of bed and excited in the morning? What would I do even if I didn't get paid?"

There are so many people that go to their jobs every morning because their neighbors are doing it and their friends are doing it. As we were instructed by our teachers from an early age, we conform to what everyone else does. There is no reason for that. I literally walk twenty-five feet to my office each day. From my bedroom to my office is twenty-five feet. This was a goal that I set for myself, and I worked hard to accomplish it at a relatively young age. This is just one example of something I wanted. What is it that you want? I have sacrificed and I have worked hard, and I was able to pull it off, contrary to what I was told by others. You can do it too!

Here's another example. Take a look at your career right now. The fact that you are reading this book is a proactive step, so I'm going to assume that you are good at what you do. Now think of this; if you took somebody like yourself, who had a base-line of skills and knowledge, you could train them to do what you do. I'm not saying they have to be a clone, but it is someone whom you could train to operate to your specifications. If you train them to do something the way you do it, and people like how you do things, then you could make money from them doing it too.

Do you see where I'm going with this? This will allow you to spend more time in pursuit of other goals and make more money in the process. The beauty of it is, you can apply this to all areas of your life. You can't always do everything yourself; sometimes you need to surround yourself with a team in order to expand your capabilities, and you do this by leveraging their talents. I'm not saying it has to be at the outset of your endeavor, but it can be incorporated somewhere down the line. You don't have to work a 9 to 5 job that you hate forever, you can create your own sources of income and fulfillment.

As you progress, keep your eyes on the road in front of you. Live your life in the way that you ultimately want it to be, not in the way that it has been or as it exists currently. You must recognize that you already have what you need. You have unlimited potential. Exercise your gifts and abilities as you so choose. Do not let others dictate your reality. Regardless of what others have told you in the past, and may continue to tell you moving ahead, you are responsible for your future. You must take action and create the life that you truly want.

CHAPTER 1
COMPLETE PARALYSIS

Things do not happen. Things are made to happen.
John F. Kennedy

• What has transpired in the past is irrelevant to your future achievements.

• We are born with limitless potential that can be tapped at any time.

• You must refuse to blindly accept the opinions of others.

• What you become isn't dependent on who you are, how much money you have or what kind of education you have.

• You can choose your life and create what you want.

• Reject thoughts and ideas that limit what you believe is possible.

• Growth is critical to fulfillment in business, career, relationships and all areas of life.

CHAPTER 2

CREATE YOUR OWN ECONOMY

Whatever course you decide upon, there is always someone to tell you that you are wrong. There are always difficulties arising which tempt you to believe that your critics are right. To map out a course of action and follow it to an end requires courage.
Ralph Waldo Emerson

Have you ever noticed how the Chairman of the Federal Reserve of the United States is cautious and appears to communicate in code? Alan Greenspan was famous for it. I am not suggesting any untoward behavior or ulterior motives, but any time the Chairman of the Federal Reserve makes a public statement it is said shrouded in mystery and ambiguity. Why is that? He knows that his words have consequences. If he telegraphs his thinking in an obvious way, or if his language is too overt, he knows he can have a direct and dramatic impact on the world markets. Investors are listening intently for any signs that help them determine what they should do.

This is not unlike the general population, always listening to talking heads in the media, friends, family and colleagues to tell them how they should interpret information and what they should do about it. At any given point in time, you are being bombarded with information about the current state of the economy and you are given the idea that it is either 'good' or 'bad.' You are told where and when to invest, which sectors are failing and what it means for you. There are times when it seems half of the experts are predicting the next bull market, while the other half are sounding the alarm, declaring a current crisis and projecting more doom and gloom well into the future. True, there are a lot of highly qualified and intelligent reporters, analysts and economists out there. But the fact is that if they had all the answers, they would likely be on a beach somewhere enjoying their riches and not chasing the numbers trying to make sense of it all, and telling you what to do.

My point is that you must evaluate conditions for yourself, and determine how those conditions do or do not affect you. You must get all the facts before you simply accept what you read in the newspaper, on the internet, and what you watch on TV. No matter what is going on in the world, in your particular country or in your own hometown, you decide how you live. In short, you create your own economy every day and just because someone else thinks things are bad, doesn't mean they have to be for you. You have to look at your specific situation and weigh the information accordingly. It is true that the world economy has suffered recently and you must proceed with this in mind, but that does not mean blindly accepting as your reality, a broad statement about the current state of things. You have the power to create opportunities for yourself, and address your own unique set of circumstances and goals at any point, no matter what the world economy is doing. You see, if you really want to be wealthy, then you can be, regardless of what anyone else may say or what the state of the economy is. This is a fact!

This applies to all areas of your life and all areas of business; though you will invariably find that other people are defining the possibilities for you under any given set of circumstances. Even if you meet up with friends for a quick meal after work at the local restaurant, you will likely be evaluated and told what you can and cannot accomplish in their opinions. Although they may mean well, these thoughts often come from people who may have let others determine their own fate. People have a tendency to want to discourage you from branching out because it is a threat to their way of existence. The other factor is, frankly, sheer ignorance. Too often people will become lazy and not expend the necessary effort to understand the true reality of possibilities. They don't have all of the facts. And of course, they don't want you to make them look bad.

Let's say that you are planning to make a change and find a more suitable home for your family. You decide to share your plan with one of your friends. In response, you may hear something similar to the following: "That's crazy. I read in the newspaper today that the housing market is terrible. You can't make a move under these current conditions." Why is this a potentially damaging response? Ask yourself what the real facts are. While it may be true that the overall housing market has slowed in some areas, do you know if that is the case for your city? Your town? Your neighborhood? It is common sense for anyone who understands the basics of economics, that even if a particular sector is suffering, like real estate, that it would also be true that there would be good deals out there as a result. Isn't it likely that prices would be lower? Wouldn't interest rates also be typically lower? Don't you think that these circumstances might enable you to potentially obtain a home (perhaps a second) at a great price, with a favourable interest rate? If you were to take advantage of these positive market conditions, wouldn't this immensely benefit you and your family? How about renting? Is it possible that you could rent your current home, generating some cash flow that will help you take care of your new mortgage, leaving yourself with a better bottom line and stronger asset base in the long run? The reality is this: You have to do what is right for you and your family. Even if the experts are telling us that the economy is on the lower end of the scale, there are always *opportunities* to be found. Trust me, I have been finding these gems for many years. Remember, when the majority of people are heading in one direction, you may seriously want to consider exploring going in the opposite direction, that is usually where you will find the best opportunities.

You must change how you think, and view what is going on around you. You must ask questions similar to the ones above, rather than just blindly accepting what others are saying. It is amazing how often we refuse to think for ourselves. There are too many people with the mindset of the friend in the above examples, who just readily accepts the headlines without digging down into the details to search for the truth, or chose to create their own wealth. You may in fact be missing out on a tremendous amount of opportunities, that remain hidden somewhere beneath the rhetoric and rubbish. Always keep at the forefront, that this applies to all areas of life and business. Your job is to be vigilant and seek all of the facts. Do not let others do your thinking for you. Stay alert, monitor changes and make adjustments to your strategy as you move forward, but always make sure to put the time in to get the real facts, and decide for yourself. You will be surprised at what you find, and you will put yourself in the best position to succeed. Do not be afraid to create your own economy in all areas of life and business.

I met with an organization recently, and I have to give them all the credit in the world for their outlook. They understand the realities of a tough economic climate, but they are gathering the necessary information to put things into perspective. The decision-makers are performing their due diligence rather than making any rash decisions. They don't make things out to be worse than they really are. They get the facts, seek opportunity and respond appropriately. You must understand that there is a lot of hype out there. This company is not just accepting that the world is about to come to an end in their sector, closing their doors and discontinuing the pursuit of their goals. They are keeping things in check and making wise and timely moves in order to continue to grow their business. They are creating their own future and economy. They are investing in their employees and asking themselves: "What is the opportunity presented in this situation?" There is always opportunity. It's up to you to find it.

I have another client who, even though he is inundated with information on a broad scale to the contrary, his company is doing fantastic. Despite a softening in the overall economy in recent years, he is taking his business to new heights, going against what others perceive to be possible. This individual had a business that was about six weeks from bankruptcy when he called me and said, "Can we talk?" I now have a letter dated about a month and a half ago from him where he said, "I want to thank you for helping me out. My business is prospering. I am healthy, and my family is happy because I spend time with them."

Things are going very well for him, but you would never know it was possible by reading the paper. While it's true that there are many people who are still suffering out there, you don't have to automatically resign yourself to the same fate, because of what you hear. You can resolve to be like my client who took control of his own situation and put himself on the road to prosperity. Sometimes you just need to take a moment, assess the situation and give yourself a chance to see things more clearly. Often, that's all it takes. Don't forget, as with all aspects of life, accountability is the key.

I think this is the true value of coaching, in that it gives you the opportunity to see your situation from an entirely new, and positive, perspective. Additionally, you are accountable to your coach. Rather than focusing on the doom and gloom, we specifically focus on the possibilities and opportunities. Understand that I didn't just talk with my client about his business, although that was a big part of it. But there is more to living a life of fulfillment than turning things around with your job or your career or making millions of dollars. There is a synergy between one's professional and personal life. There is, or should be, a balance. It's a fact that you cannot be truly successful in your professional life or your career until you are first successful, at least at some level, in your personal life. What my client and I were able to do, was work together to move him to the point where he is now able to balance his personal life along with his business; he has found that synergy. Though this client owns and operates a business, he now spends quality time with his family rather than being at the office eighteen hours a day. You would be surprised how much this can invigorate a person. By shifting some attention to his family, his business made an incredible leap. He created his own economy by devoting more time to that which is most important in his life. The path is different for each of us. That is why you must make your own way and not listen to detractors.

Prior to establishing my current consulting, coaching and speaking business, I owned and operated a firm in the legal field. My personal shift began when I was asked by an immigrant couple to help them through some legal matters. Being new to North America, they struggled with English as their second language, and needed someone to help guide them along. I initially declined, as I didn't want to become involved in the kind of work that they were asking me to assist them with. They were insistent and I eventually relented and accepted their file. In the end, it was an extremely rewarding experience. I was able to successfully help them navigate through their challenges, and they were enormously grateful.

I tell this story because this episode was the catalyst in my creating and building a hugely successful business. Something was created from nothing. I was able to launch into a whole new business venture as a result of this experience. I created my own economy. I started with one client, and from that client's referral, one expanded into two then two created four, then eight and so on. By the time I sold that business in August of 2007, I had a full contingent of staff and an office, and I was making a great deal of money. I was creating my own wealth! The mindset of creating my own economy didn't stop when I started the business. It continued for the duration of ownership, right up until I sold it. Truth be told, I live my live that way.

Different businesses operate with unique business models and in countless different approaches. You can build a business without a great deal of money, or without spending a large amount on traditional advertising. Not all businesses work this way, in this particular instance, this business grew entirely from word of mouth. If I provided a great service for a client, they referred me to friends, family, associates, and others.

Life and business are all about making personal connections and building relationships. You see, it's all about people, and so often I think we forget this. This is applicable in your life, your business, your career and your relationships. If you always remember this and provide a good, valuable and needed service, it will pay you huge dividends. Here is something for you to ponder, the previous story and what I alluded to after is proof that if you focus on your clients and what is important, the money will take care of itself. Its been said that, "It's not about the money."

I know of real estate agents that spend $60,000 each month in advertising. They have effectively bought themselves a job, and are so focused on attracting clients, that they dump money into gimmicks rather than satisfying their current customers and building a referral stream. If they were to stop advertising, people would think they were out of business. This is a tremendous mistake in my opinion. They are convinced that advertising is the way to go because that is what everyone else in the industry is doing, and once they start, they are typically unable to stop. They become stuck in a vicious cycle. This also applies to life. We get ourselves locked into a vicious cycle of listening to others and accepting what they say, rather than focusing on what is best for us. Whether it is running a small business or a large corporation, you must create your own economy by putting forth your best effort in whatever you are doing. By addressing the needs of others and helping them solve problems you will receive wonderful recommendations in return.

I evolved into this kind of work—and I am writing this book as part of that goal—for a simple reason: I want to be able to share with as many people as possible the message of infinite potential. Sure, money is a requirement, lifestyle is a priority, but more importantly, I want to spread the message that we all have the power inside of us—right now—to create the lives we seek. The power isn't something you must attain from an outside source; it already exists within you.

Every single one of us has infinite and amazing potential. The problem is that we limit ourselves by simply failing to recognize this potential, and by permitting fear to cripple us, thus limiting our abilities. You may not even be aware that you are putting these restrictions on yourself. As you read this book, I will help you open this awareness and see areas in your life that you didn't even realize were being affected.

It comes down to awareness, and awareness is knowledge. You must first be aware that the power to change your life already resides within you. My goal is to move as many people as I can to action, to inspire as many people as I can to grow, and to hold you accountable. I firmly believe that if more people had the awareness and the knowledge that they have limitless potential, we would see an impact that would resonate around the globe. You have the ability to make a tremendous difference not only in your own life, but in the lives of others throughout the world. We are anxiously awaiting your unique, special contributions. Step forth and share the power of your gifts with yourself, and with others.

As Wallace D. Wattles stresses in his fantastic book, *The Science of Getting Rich*, you have to approach life with an open mind. You cannot allow yourself to dissect everything to death, or reject ideas before you really even consider them. Sometimes you just have to let go and accept reality, but you must never blindly accept what detractors may attempt to impose upon you. Open yourself up to the truth. Gather the critical information that is all around you, and make your own determination about the opportunities that are so abundant in any given set of circumstances.

I receive a fair number of emails from people saying, "I've watched the movie, *The Secret*, but I am still struggling. Can you help me? I've been to all the seminars and read all the books, but the Law of Attraction isn't working for me.

I'm not getting what I want in my life. I've set goals and I have yet to achieve them. It's not happening for me. What do I do?" I understand their frustration. Millions of people have seen The Secret and it has been a phenomenal starting point, but the problem is that it is only a starting point as it leaves out several critical pieces of the puzzle. There is more to getting what you want from life than just deciding and focusing your thoughts on something. This is the Law of Attraction and while it is very powerful, there is also more to it than that. Here is a hint for you, "The Power of A."

Some ideas take time to manifest in your life, and timing is everything. If you blindly push toward a goal, you may actually defeat yourself. You must be aware that your particular path may be slower or faster, but that it will happen when the time is right. There is a principle called the Law of Gender, which states that there is an unknown time-period required for an idea to become mature. In other words, it takes time for your ideas to come to fruition. You must exercise a measure of patience and gather the knowledge and tools you need to become successful while working toward that goal. You don't decide to climb a mountain and then suddenly appear at the top. You must gather the necessary tools and make steady progress to reach your goal. That being said, there is something called the Quantum Leap, and we delve into this phenomenon in one of our mentorship programs.

It is crucial that you understand how important it is to take action, even in baby steps, toward your goal. You can't sit on the couch eating potato chips and expect to attract the life you want! You have to get up and get it. In order to get something, you have to make a sustained effort; you have to make some sacrifice (in most cases, that will be time); and most importantly, you have to act in specific ways toward your goal. Without action, your goals are meaningless. You must put forth the effort to transform your goals into reality.

The other critical component that is frequently overlooked is, that you also have to give more than you get. Look at it this way: If you are a professional billing at $100/hour, you want to always make sure that you are providing a value that exceeds that hourly rate. You want to always be giving that little extra value to your client. Too often, we go through life with an ugly refrain, an inward focus of: "Me, me, me; Want, want, want." And then we can't understand why others aren't handing us everything we desire. It's true that those who give, get, but there is more to the equation. Your giving must be authentic; it must come from the heart and the soul. If we have genuinely ingrained this sentiment into our true nature, and we are not trying to exploit this rule for selfish gain, then you will find truth in the giving statement, and will receive accordingly.

You can't just get up in the morning and say, "Okay, I really want to be more successful, so I guess I am going to donate to a charity today so I can get something in return." It doesn't work that way. If that is your approach, you will find that you will likely get nothing at all. If you approach your life, and your business, from a place that is true, I guarantee that you will start seeing results and opportunities that you could never have anticipated.

Creating your own economy is a result of several ideas. First and foremost, it is starting where you are today, in the present. Your career and your life may not be exactly where you want them at this moment, and that's okay. Let it go and don't dwell on the shoulda, coulda, woulda ideas that drag you down. The big picture for you may be a little way off in the distance. Such is the case for many of us. Life is a journey. You must learn to embrace it. You can't let the thought of a mysterious journey keep you from setting sail – instead it must be approached as an adventure. Action is a key part of reaching your destination. Don't wait for perfection or for circumstances to change before you start, things will never be perfect and circumstance will never be right. You must start from where you are, and do everything you can today. Create a goal. Visualize it; live it; make it your reality. Follow the advice of Napoleon Hill which is that if you make it a near obsession and a burning desire, it will happen. It is that burning desire that will sustain you through life's inevitable obstacles. Again, you must start and do the best job that you can from where you are today. The rest will fall into place. Always keep your mind on the big picture, and the smaller goals will be achieved along the way, just like taking steps up a mountain. You must persist and have faith.

Creating your own economy also has a lot to do with your dedication—whether the state of things at first glance seems positive or negative. It is all a matter of perspective. It's up to you to interpret the available information, and find the opportunities that will lead you closer to your goals. You can and will make changes throughout your life, but that should not stop you from always putting your best effort forward, giving the maximum value. Whether you own a business, or whether you work for somebody else, it doesn't matter. Always perform at your optimum level and do your best to continually improve.

You can achieve any goal that you set for yourself. Will it be easy? Perhaps not. Are there things you must know before you embark on your journey? Sure. Are there business processes and procedures of which you will need to be aware? Absolutely. If you have a goal in mind, you must start now, do not wait. The rest will fall into place. We will talk more about goals in chapters seven and eight, but you have to ask yourself, "What do you want to achieve in life? What is it that you really want? What is it that you are passionate about?" Once you have made that discovery, creating your own economy will become easier.

Be mindful that there are certainly no shortage of opinions out there, and no shortage of people that will be happy to share those opinions with you. Your job is to decipher the vast amount of information that is flowing in through your senses and influencing your decisions. Your specific dreams require specific actions in order to convert them into the reality that you see for yourself.

Keep in mind that each person has their own reality. They are contending with their own circumstances and have their own agenda. Again, I don't want to ascribe any ulterior motives to well-intentioned individuals, but you have to have a filter, understanding that what is being conveyed comes from a source of imperfect knowledge. We all have biases and flaws. That is why it is so critical to assess each situation individually, and properly evaluate all information, making necessary adjustments to achieve your own particular ambitions and aspirations.

If you want to live the life of your dreams, if you are unsatisfied with your current situation and with the direction you are heading, then you must alter your course. You must use the most valuable tool in your arsenal. If you want to change your results, you have to change your mind.

CHAPTER 2
CREATE YOUR OWN ECONOMY

You are never too old to set another goal or to dream a new dream.
C. S. Lewis

• Don't buy into the media's tales of gloom or doom.

• Open your mind to what you really want in life, and allow yourself to dream.

• Make a conscious effort to refuse to focus on the negative.

• Action is a key component to creating the life you want.

• You can create your own economy in any economic time and in any situation.

• Be an achiever and find the opportunities.

• Shifting your perceptions is key to seeing what life really has to offer.

• Give maximum value in all areas of your life and you will be rewarded for your efforts.

CHAPTER 3

CHANGE YOUR MIND, CHANGE YOUR RESULTS

We can't solve problems by using the same kind of thinking we used when we created them.
Albert Einstein

So now that we have identified some of the most common obstacles preventing you from setting off on the road to all that you truly desire, we have reached the crucial component in our lesson, and that is understanding your mind. The title of this book is *Change Your Mind, Change Your Results* and it is a significant concept. This idea is so potent that it should be the constant refrain that drives you throughout each day of your personal and professional lives. It is not a new concept either. In fact, there has been universal agreement upon this central idea among virtually every great thinker throughout recorded history. It is not a complicated philosophy. In fact, its beauty lies in its simplicity.

This power of your mind will be the central focus of this chapter, and is woven into every aspect of the book. If you can accept that we become what we think about, then it should be relatively easy to deduce that if you are unhappy with where you are, or where you have been, then you need to focus on something dramatically different. You may be thinking, "It can't be that simple." As far as a strategy is concerned it is, but you still have to take action. I am not suggesting that your path will be without perceived difficulties, far from it. You will most definitely face road blocks, but you must know that even subtle changes in the way you think will have dramatic and lasting results on your life. Also as previously stated, accountability is key. Be accountable to yourself and to someone that is going to keep you accountable. I suggest a Strategic Accountability Coach.

We already know that our future is a direct result of the thoughts we have today. We also know that whatever we concentrate on will manifest as our reality. Grasping this principle is the starting point that will help you go from a place of mediocre and dismal results, to a haven of wonderful potential, phenomenal opportunity and most importantly extraordinary results. By changing the way you think, you will completely reshape every aspect of your life. Altering your thought process is the catalyst to bring about all of the things in your life that once seemed only a dream way off in the distance.

Think of it this way, if you know that everything you see around you is a result of past thoughts, and you continue to think in the same way that you always have, what can you expect for your future? The answer is obvious, isn't it? You will see the same results. If you become what you think about, then it only makes sense that where you are today is a direct result of your previous thoughts. If you are like the majority of people, you have developed limiting habitual thinking that continues to put you in the same predicaments repeatedly. So naturally, if you want to experience different results, you must change your way of thinking; the way that has led to the unsatisfactory results that you may now be experiencing.

You have probably heard that the definition of insanity is, doing the same things over and over again and expecting different results. Well, the same idea applies here. You cannot possibly expect to achieve better results if you continue to think and behave in the way that you always have in the past. You have to break free from the same old way of thinking that keeps putting you back into your current state of unhappiness. We see people stuck in these cycles all around us—in our everyday lives, in our careers and businesses.

For example; take the senior executive who has worked for many years in one industry or profession. He likely doesn't spring out of bed eager for new opportunities like he once did, in fact his life feels like a never ending treadmill – no real highs or lows. It's not a bad life at all, and it's not that he's necessarily complaining, but he's bored and really misses being excited by what he spends his days doing. Perhaps he thinks about being an entrepreneur, and striking out on his own to meet the needs of prospective clients his current company is ignoring. Of course, the first thing that will fill his head are the same ideas that keep him where he is, i.e. "This is a great job with benefits – I don't want to just throw that away. What if I fail, how will I hold my head up? I'm just not all that crazy about working day and night again like I used to, in order to launch a new endeavor."

It is this type of thinking that can convince the executive, business owner or anyone to just keep running on their own personal treadmill, not really loving their life, but not willing to risk getting off either. No one convinces us we have to do or be anything – we convince ourselves. You can recreate your life at any time or at any moment, you just have to decide to open your mind to new ways of thinking about yourself and what you really want. Don't get caught up in placing the blame on others. How many times have you heard someone say, "Well I can't consider that kind of change, I have a family to support." Or "Well I have all this experience or education in this area and that would be wasted if I suddenly went an entirely new direction." Neither of these statements are obstacles, they are merely excuses.

Although the concept is easy to understand in theory, I'm not going to mislead you and tell you that it is always going to be easy to adapt and think differently about your life, or what you can accomplish. You will have to gather information, work hard and make tough decisions. You will have to make sacrifices to change. The choice to change, or not, is yours alone. Are you willing to modify your approaches and thought processes in order to get what you really want instead of staying on the same old treadmill? I know it may seem like leaping off a tall cliff, but you must break free from your fears and understand that your perception of the risk is just that - perception. Perception is not reality. Once you take the first step, it seems a much easier undertaking. If you are looking to improve your life, you must approach things differently than you have in the past, and you must face these perceptions in order to redefine or recreate them.

If you understand that the past does not equal the future, you know that you have the capability to change and experience anything you want in life. Do you have the desire to do so? I am frequently amazed at the level of unhappiness or boredom people will endure in their lives just because they don't really have a passion or desire to do anything else. Time is a thief, and it passes by almost without notice if we are not acutely aware of what we are experiencing. When you choose to become aware, your perspective of time alters, and instead of living like you have all the time in the world, you begin to realize that time is your most valuable commodity. You can't make more of it and you can't get it back once it's gone. As you really grasp this idea, then every minute becomes more precious than the last and you completely lose the desire to spend even one more day not living your dreams.

I know a restaurant owner who was extremely unhappy with his occupation. He had owned and managed a particular restaurant for eight years and worked very long hours. He felt tied to his work and rarely got a chance to travel, or even get away for a weekend. He constantly thought about changing occupations, but he was so good at his job, and so used to it, that it was hard for him to see a future in any other industry or profession. Inevitably, he opened then closed three more restaurants over the next six years. He would start a new restaurant thinking that this time it would be different, but after about 18 months it would turn out exactly the same, and he would become bored and restless again. When he talked about doing something in another field, those who knew him would raise a brow and question why he would change professions when he so obviously was well suited to what he was doing. This outside criticism each time convinced him to settle for opening another restaurant.

Finally after many years and four tries at making himself happy, he changed the way he thought. In order to get into a new occupation, he had to create a different experience and find what he was really passionate about. He had been an amateur photographer for years, so he purchased a new camera and got serious about making this passion his livelihood. He started part time while still working his restaurants but then as time went on, he won a few awards and the assignments started to flood in. He used all those years of customer service skills to great advantage, and soon built a solid network of editors who regularly gave him premium work. Nine years later he travels the globe photographing some of the most famous locations and sites in the world and guess what - he loves what he does. If he'd never changed the way he thought about himself, and what he wanted, he might still be boiling pasta or flipping burgers and completely miserable.

Change your mind, change your results is altering the way we perceive everything in our lives. You certainly don't have to make any sweeping shifts right off the bat, but you must start with small changes. When I am conducting a seminar, I advise people to take three seconds and collect their thoughts as they are processing any situation. It's not a long period of time. Just think about what you are going to do before you do it, and what the ramifications may be. This is an example of a minor change that anyone can make. Instead of letting your emotions override your reactions, don't talk; don't react in anyway. Just take three seconds and think before you speak or respond. This simple maneuver can lead to tremendous results in business and in your personal relationships. Respond rather than reacting.

Some time ago, upon returning from a wonderful and relaxing Caribbean holiday with my wife, we learned that my wife's grandmother was in neighboring town for a visit. We immediately made a decision to drive the 35 minutes to pay a visit. While making a right turn on a red light at an intersection, another driver had proceeded through a yellow light and almost rear ended me. It was a pretty close call, but realizing these things happen sometimes on the road, I didn't give it much more thought and went on our way.

When I turned into a nearby service station, I realized that the other driver involved in the incident had pulled in behind me. This person got out of his car, came up to the window of my vehicle and told me, in no uncertain terms, and in very colorful language, what he thought of me and my driving abilities—a classic case of road rage. He also wanted me to get out of my car and discuss the situation. It was springtime so it was warm out, and my window was down. After he was finished his tirade, I looked out at him and I said, "I am sorry if I offended you in any way. Thank you for your advice, I will try to do better next time." Well the driver from the other car was not buying this at all. This did not calm him down one bit; he kept up his antics: yelling, screaming and pointing his finger in my face. He said, "The next time you make a turn in that circumstance, you should do it this way." And he proceeded to give me a driving lesson. I again said, "Thank you, I appreciate your advice." The moral of the story is that this situation could have escalated and become much worse. This is important. If you react, you have relinquished control to the other party or the situation. If you respond, after exercising the three second rule, you retain control. Who or what is controlling you?

I could have just reacted in the story above and both of us would likely have ended up in a fist fight, but what did I do by approaching the situation in this way? Well for starters, I took the wind out of his sails. I refused to perpetuate the argument, exacerbate the situation, or let it escalate any further. I didn't allow him, or the situation, to control me or my reaction. I remained in control. So what did he do? He walked back to his car muttering expletives at me under his breath. Unless he was willing to resort to violence, there was nothing else he could do. I took control of the situation.

Instead of getting out of my vehicle and saying, "You son-of-a-you-know-what, let's go," surely resulting in unnecessary violence. I took three seconds and thought about my response. I allowed myself that extra time to keep calm. I cannot claim to always be on my best behavior, but in this situation, I suppressed my initial and natural instinct that was telling me to give it right back to the other driver. I changed my mind, and certainly changed my results.

How would you react in a situation like that? Are you happy with the results that you are getting in your life? Are you constantly allowing somebody else, or a situation, to control your life or to control what you think? To control how you react? No matter the situation, changing your mind—and ultimately how you control your mind—changes your results. I changed the results of that traffic situation, by allowing myself three seconds to maintain my composure. I was happy with the results. If I would have gotten out and told the other gentleman where to go and how to get there, we would have surely come to blows. Would it have been worth it?

My point is not to convey myself as righteous or like I have everything figured out. I have learned a great deal in my life, and know from personal experience that it works. I don't just spout theory and how things 'should' be. I know for a fact that these principles work, and I'm only sharing those techniques that I have utilized myself.

The traffic incident is just one small example. We haven't even scratched the surface of all the areas that this new awareness can affect. Take a moment to reflect on some of your habits. Ask yourself the following questions as they relate to each paradigm: "Am I happy with my current results? What could I do differently in order to make improvements?" Really dig deep. Be honest with yourself. As I have said, this is not necessarily going to be easy. It will require some soul searching and some hard work. You may not always like the answers to the questions that you ask of yourself, but that should never stop you from asking them. You must take responsibility for your thoughts, as well as the feelings and actions that follow. It is all part of the learning process. In changing your mind, not only will you be changing your results, but you will open yourself up to a new world of discovery and growth. You will be rewarded with a sense of fulfillment unlike any you have ever felt or experienced.

This is not a onetime activity either. Evaluating your actions and deciding where you are going, is a constant process that involves far reaching and big picture goals. Whether it is with respect to your career or your professional life, are you really focused on what you want long term? Or are you focused on little day-to-day things? We alluded to this earlier, but you cannot let yourself be easily distracted by mundane details that really have no relevance to your larger aspirations. It's up to you to remain focused and on target. You may have slipped into a pattern that is keeping you bogged down in the current state of things. This happens on occasion, but you have to become aware of these patterns and make changes to free yourself from their confines. Make every move a productive one that propels you in the direction of your goals.

Let me give you another example. I mentioned that I recently returned from a vacation. During this period of time, I spent the majority of my time outside enjoying the weather. If I happened to be in my hotel room and I wanted to be inspired by the wonderful scenery, I would invariably look out the window at the ocean. If I narrowed my focus and was only concerned with what was directly in front of me, all I would see is little spots on the glass from the sea spray in the air. While maybe temporarily interesting, it would ultimately not give me that feeling of inspiration, which is why I took the vacation in the first place!

If you have a goal, you have to broaden your focus, and look beyond what is directly in front of you in order to fully appreciate the beauty. When I broadened my focus, I was able to see the beautiful blue-green water and the sunrise on the horizon. My point is that you cannot become so bogged down by what is right in front of you at any given time, that it prevents you from seeing the bigger picture, in this case, the sunrise.

When you truly focus on those broad ideas and goals that are important in your life, don't forget that you must act! Execution is at times the component that we miss, don't miss out on your dreams.

Your dreams will remain out of reach, unless you take the specific steps necessary to achieve them. The journey begins with the all important component of changing your mind, but it continues by moving forward. Many people try something, and give up. Don't try, just start right now and begin building momentum. Those who try, never succeed. You are capable of extraordinary things. Don't ever forget that no matter who you are or where you come from, you can always improve your current state, improve yourself, and improve the lives of those most important to you.

When I am giving a seminar, I always ask people this question: "Do you want to change the results you are currently getting?" The response is uniform. Everyone agrees: Yes they do. Why else would they be in attendance, right? I then like to make this statement: "Raise your hand if you believe you are successful." The response here varies, but generally about two thirds of the hands in the room go up. I follow with this question: "How many of you believe you could be more successful than you are right now?" And it's funny. The same two thirds of the hands go up. This has always been fascinating to me. Everybody—I don't care who it is— you, me or anyone else—can be more successful. The fact that the same one third that isn't successful now, also don't believe they can be more successful in the future, is indicative of their limiting mindset and prior conditioning.

From the least fortunate to the middle class to millionaires and even billionaires, everyone has the ability to become more successful. This is where the change in mindset comes into play. Just acknowledging this fact, and deciding to do something about it will put you on the road to prosperity and present opportunities that you never could have envisioned.

There is no reason to limit yourself wherever you fall in the spectrum of achievement and fulfillment, and you don't necessarily have to do it all on your own. It's okay to seek council and guidance from those that have been there before you. Even the elite athletes and most advanced thinkers have coaches and mentors. This should tell you something. They know that their perspective can get skewed on occasion, and they are not shy about asking for help to reach their goals. They utilize the gifts and strengths of others, in conjunction with their own, and then consistently move forward.

I have personally helped people achieve extraordinary things, from improving their lives to doubling their income in a year. It can be done. I don't care who you are; the transformation can happen. First you must make a fundamental change in the way you look at things. You must change your mind. You must want it! If you are one of those people who doubt their abilities, the first step on your road to prosperity is to understand the importance of your thoughts, and the power of the mind. In order to really grasp how important it is, I've devoted the next chapter to understanding how your mind works. This is a necessary foundation for you to establish, in order to fully experience and harness the power of your mind. Even if you don't believe you can completely change your life right this second, I challenge you to keep reading and I will prove it.

You can achieve anything you want to, and it takes no more energy to dream big. Napoleon Hill states that "what the mind can conceive and believe, it can achieve." Take that little spark of hope and follow along, and I will teach you the exact steps to have the personal and professional life of your dreams.

CHAPTER 3
CHANGE YOUR MIND, CHANGE YOUR RESULTS

Always bear in mind that your own resolution to succeed is more important than any other.
Abraham Lincoln

- Your mind is incredibly powerful.

- Your thoughts create your life. Yesterday created today and today creates tomorrow.

- If you keep doing what you have always done, you will get the same results.

- Change happens all around us and we must change with it, you choose if that change moves you forward or keeps you in the same place.

- Everything starts with awareness and expands as you consciously make choices rather than just floating through the same old routine.

- The smartest people in the world seek guidance and counseling to move themselves forward in their lives.

CHAPTER 4

THE POWER OF YOU

All that you accomplish or fail to accomplish with your life is the direct result of your thoughts.
James Allen

What we think about and dwell on each day plays a crucial role in our results. In order to understand this connection and then leverage it to enhance the opportunities we encounter on a daily basis, it is important to understand how powerful our thoughts are, and how little we understand about how our minds work.

This is a critical piece of the puzzle as you move forward into new territory in pursuit of your strategic objectives and goals. In order to enhance any skill, you must first understand the fundamentals of how and why that skill works, and yes, thinking is a skill! You have power over your thoughts, it's just that most people aren't aware of, or don't exercise, that power or pay attention to what their thoughts are focused on.

Most of us can essentially meander our way, from an intellectual standpoint, through the educational system, from elementary school all the way on up through to the collegiate level, and yet never be taught how to think. I don't mean that we didn't learn our ABC's or that $1 + 1 = 2$, I'm talking about how to think creatively and use our minds effectively. Of course there are some that naturally learn to focus their minds – often through experiential activities such as sports or business, which force you to set and achieve goals. This requires a shift in your thinking, an out of the box and dramatically different approach. Those not fortunate enough to have these experiences, or to fully utilize the lessons learned in other areas of life, may be at a disadvantage when it comes to taking their lives to new level. You see friends, most people today, likely around 95% will fail to achieve their goals and objectives. Why you ask, there are a few reasons, but primarily because they fail to set the right goals and take action. Every move you make needs to be productive!

The good news is that these skills can be learned and enhanced no matter your age or current experience level. Absolutely anyone from a child, all the way to an octogenarian can improve their ability to use their minds more effectively, and to its greatest advantage. We can learn to evaluate opportunities quickly, think strategically and project great outcomes. It is a constant learning and growing process that only stops when we stop paying attention or become complacent.

If we do stop paying attention, we may find ourselves temporarily stymied and seemingly unable to dig out of the rut that we believe that we've fallen into. As a result, most of us find our thoughts drifting aimlessly, because we are unaware of the limitless potential that resides within us, or of the methods by which we can release or tap into it.

Thinking is the highest function that we can perform, and it is what separates humans from the rest of life forms on our planet. Thought is what creates and imagines what our lives can be, and brings it into being. Whether it is the chair you are sitting in, the home you live in, or the car that you drive to work each day, all were nothing but a thought in the mind of a person before eventually securing a place in reality. This is a powerful concept when you realize that you can change the direction of the world, with just an idea. For example, it's reasonable to believe that Bill Gates, while tinkering with the beginnings of his personal computer idea in college, had no idea that his concept would change the way we live and function in today's world. Yet he believed in the idea and as each milestone was reached, dared to imagine the next. This is how greatness happens – one thought at a time.

In order to truly understand how thoughts enhance our ability to reach our goals, you must understand that we think in pictures. When we hear a word, we immediately search for, and hold an image of that object in our minds, just as if it were on a movie screen. Try this for yourself right now - think of a feather, a bird, or a house, you will see a picture of that object on the screen of your mind. You don't see the words "feather," "bird" or "house." You actually see an image of a feather, a bird or a house and while we each may see a slightly different version of these items, the fact that we see pictures applies to all things, no matter what we are thinking about. The clearer the picture we have in our mind, the less confusion and the more order we experience. This is an important point, because one of the key reasons people don't achieve their goals is that they don't have a clear image or vision of what exactly it is that they want to achieve. If the vision is opaque and vague, your results will be lackluster and mediocre. The clearer and more vibrant the picture, the less anxiety, doubt and fear you will experience, and the more confidence you will have as you advance in the direction of your goals.

A great example of this, is the person who says, "I want to earn more money." You might think that is a worthy goal, but it presents a number of issues. Five dollars is more money – but is that what you meant? I would guess it is not, but you can see that just wanting more money is an ambiguous goal. Now think about that goal for a minute – what picture pops into your mind? Is it mountains of money because that is what you said you wanted? Or is it a bigger house, a more luxurious car, and a better education for your children. More often than not, we want what money can buy and the options it gives us to choose how we will live. Money is essentially an idea, because it is used to get us what we want but it is not, in and of itself, what we want.

This is an example of how important it is to understand how we think. If you set a goal that you have no possibility of focusing on from a mental standpoint – like making more money – you have little hope of achieving it. However, if you focus on the life you want to live and that money can give you, then you are able to make that dream a reality. Once you really understand how to use this mental power, you are way ahead in the pursuit of your dreams.

The Mind

If thought is the highest function that we can perform as human beings, and we think in pictures, then it only stands to reason that we must have a clear picture of what our mind looks like in order to derive the full benefit of its power. If you ask most people what their mind looks like, they'll probably tell you that they see an image of the brain. While this is a natural response, in actuality, the brain is no more your mind than your knee or your elbow. The mind is not even really a *thing*, it's actually an *activity* within every cell of your body. It is also the repository of our experiences, beliefs, and our understanding of the world around us. Though nobody can truly see the mind, I am going to provide you with an illustration that will at least better enable you to conceptualize how it works.

The late Dr. Thurman Fleet was the founder of the Concept Therapy Movement. As he was working with patients afflicted with illness and disease, Dr. Fleet found that if he really wanted to augment the process of healing, he had to deal with the human being holistically, as an entire entity, rather than as a collection of various anatomical parts. He came to the conclusion that he must also interact with a person as a *spiritual* being that has been gifted with intellect and that was living in and through a *physical* body. Dr. Fleet's view was that in order for someone to begin to see a true picture of health, he had to give the patient a visual representation of what the mind looked like. The illustration below is referred to as the "stick person" and was developed by Dr. Fleet in 1934. It is not a complicated rendering, and like all great ideas is elegant and extremely effective in its simplicity.

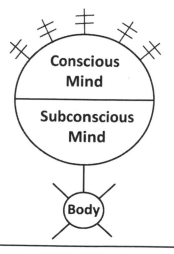

As you can see from this diagram, the mind has been separated into two parts: The conscious mind is on the top; the subconscious mind on the bottom. Our conscious mind is our thinking mind. This is where our free will and awareness resides. This area is the center of our ability to choose, and we can to choose anything we want. We can choose our own thoughts, or we can choose to allow other people to think for us and tell us what to expect. We can expose ourselves to conversations, watch television and observe the news and allow that to control what we think about, or we can exercise our ability to craft our own thoughts and seek answers or solutions to challenges. Keep in mind, that as we have already discussed, we become what we think about.

As adults, we have the ability to accept, reject, or neglect any information that comes into our conscious mind. Think about this for a moment, it's your call, your decision and therefore anything that you allow in, will become a part of you.

Here is how it works. The moment that you make a decision to accept a thought or idea into your conscious mind, it automatically becomes impressed upon the sub-conscious mind. Everything that you allow into your conscious mind is because you permitted it in by making that decision to accept it. Your sub-conscious mind is your power center and the God-like part of you that brings it all together. It is where everything is stored. It's also extremely important to know that both internally or externally generated thoughts or feelings will impact your results.

For a child, however, *everything* goes in. A child does not have the ability to reject the wide range of information to which they are exposed during their all-important impressionable years. That is precisely the reason that small children, upon hearing a specific word, a word perhaps not intended for small ears, will pick it up and repeat it frequently. They have, unfortunately, not yet developed their filter as to what is acceptable behavior and what is not. The ability to make decisions and choose is present, but not yet completely developed. There is no way for them to stop what goes into their subconscious mind by way of the conscious mind. This also presents a generationally persistent belief system issue.

As we mentioned in chapter one, a majority of the decisions that we make as adults are based upon programming or unsolicited 'gifts' that we've obtained from our parents, grandparents, religious leaders and educators. Even when we're no longer directly influenced by them, the ideas and opinions we were exposed to have become a part of our belief system and self-image and can be very difficult to change.

Our subconscious mind, on the other hand, works differently. It is our emotional mind. This is the part of us that stores all of our memories. Everything we've ever experienced in our lives has been deposited and banked here, whether you are able to recall it or not. While we have the ability and capability to filter what enters into our conscious mind as adults, we have no such power when it comes to the subconscious mind. The subconscious mind of any individual—no matter who they are—accepts whatever that individual has permitted, uncritically, into the conscious mind. In other words whatever you think is important, is what the subconscious mind is given to work on. When we don't monitor and control our thoughts, random ideas can end up in our subconscious minds that can be very damaging.

We must be aware that there is a straight and unfettered path from the conscious mind to the subconscious mind. Hence the reason for making constant decisions about the sensitivity of our filter, or what we permit into our conscious minds. All of the information that we gather through our physical senses or our abilities to see, hear, smell, taste and touch, ends up in our subconscious mind, via the conscious mind, is there indefinitely. Take a look at the stick person on page 71.

There is no way to remove it. The good news, however, is you can choose to overcome or rather replace, your existing unwanted and negative habits and paradigms. Perhaps now it is a little clearer for you, as to the reason why the subconscious mind is so important. It is the subconscious mind that actually steers our daily lives. The subconscious mind is our POWER center.

It is important to understand that the thoughts we choose will ultimately be expressed in feelings. Those feelings then produce actions, which in turn produce results. If we are serious about wanting to change our results, we have to change what's going on inside our minds. We must live from the inside out, not from the outside in. In order for you to produce a result, such as having a successful business, you must start with a thought that you can visualize on the screen of your mind. This thought must become a passion that transforms into strong feelings. It's these deep seated feelings that will be expressed through your actions, and will ultimately manifest as results. I believe it was Napoleon Hill that said something to the effect that, in order to be truly successful, your goals must become a near obsession and a burning desire.

The RESULTS formula of high achievers

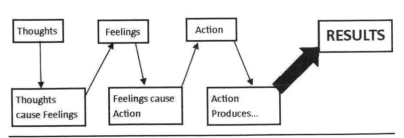

We are bombarded with thousands of images, ideas and concepts each day. If you don't consciously choose your thoughts, you are allowing what you see, hear or feel to control what occupies your mind. This means, if you spend hours watching or focusing on the opposite of positive ideas, your results will mirror your focus. If all you focus on is negativity or what you don't want, even if you say you aren't aware of it or you think you can't change the way you think, you are going to manifest in your life, in your business or career and relationships the things you don't want. For example, if you spend hours listening to all the talking heads on television talk shows about the state of the economy, how can you focus on those actions that will make you and your business successful? You are in fact, undermining your progress.

Remember this key point, truly successful and wealthy people look for and find opportunities in every situation, no matter how dire it may appear at the onset. If you are going to take advice from someone, it is important to make certain that the person you're watching or listening to is getting phenomenal results in that area of their life or business. Therefore, if you want to make positive changes in your life, you must also be cognizant of what you are allowing into your mind. You must identify harmful stimuli and limit or negate your exposure to those ideas. Instead fill the void with positive, uplifting and practical knowledge from those you really want to emulate. As we discussed earlier, we must live from the inside out, and not the outside in. We must ensure that we are inner directed and not outer directed.

Intellectual Faculties

Nearly any young child would likely be able to list the *physical* senses, as these are how we first experience the world around us. But, if we were to ask any number of college graduates to list our *intellectual faculties*, at best, most would be guessing. It makes sense that if we're not taught how powerful our thoughts are, we are also not taught how to use our minds effectively and creatively. Your intellectual faculties play a large role in how you think and will have a direct effect on your results. So let's define them.

One of the most important intellectual faculties is our *perception*. Perception is the way we view things. It's how we see things, and how we interpret them. The reason it is so important is because perception is a fluid concept. This means that we have the ability to look at any circumstance or condition, and judge it to be either positive or negative. The situation may not change, but our perception of it can change dramatically.

It was Dr. Wayne Dyer who said, "When we change the way we look at things, the things we look at change." Here's an example. Suppose you are expected to give a presentation to the board members and executive team of your corporation. You have been gearing up to present your new idea, which could potentially affect your entire career path. There is a lot riding on this presentation; there is a lot at stake. You have been working for weeks on every minute detail, and going over your material repeatedly to ensure that you have it just right. Finally, the day arrives for the meeting. Two hours before you are to give your presentation, you receive word that the CEO is unable to make it into town; he will be postponing his visit until further notice.

You may be understandably disappointed or even upset. Your internal conversation may be something like this, "I spent all this time preparing and now the meeting has been called off. I was all ready to go and now I have to wait, putting a stop to the momentum." But wait a minute. Isn't it possible that there is a silver lining in all of this? Isn't it possible that you were just given more time to work on that stubborn detail that perhaps you knew you weren't entirely ready to present? Is it possible that not only do you now have the bulk of the leg work already behind you so you can devote your time and attention to other productive efforts, but you also have more time to make your original presentation even better? Or even more persuasive? It's all a matter of perception. You can look at things in a negative light or you can look at evolving circumstances and scour them for the hidden opportunities that will lead to even better results. That is the magic of perception.

The next of the intellectual faculties is *will*. Now when we hear the word "will," we're not necessarily talking in the sense of forcing our will or our opinions upon others. What we're talking about is our ability to concentrate, to stay focused on one thing to the exclusion of all outside distractions. We are talking about your determination as it relates to pursuing any objective or goal that you set for yourself. Your will is your focused persistence and tenacity. It is your ability to stay on track, even it if means slight alterations in your course, as you venture out into foreign territory.

While you are engaged in any given endeavour, it is important that you concentrate your efforts on the end result. This will allow you to gage, and perhaps even avoid obstacles that you may encounter on your journey. You must maintain your course by focusing on the things that are in your control; so as not to dilute your resources or mental energy by spending time on those things that happened in the past or that you cannot control. You see friends, most people forget this. They focus their energy on those things that they cannot control or that took place in the past. This is not productive, and will not assist you in achieving your objectives.

Let's assume that you are heading to an important sales meeting, and on the way into the building you are denied access by the security desk. The story is that your name is not on the visitors list for the company you are supposed to be visiting . After a discussion and you insisting that there was an error, it all turned out to be an innocent misunderstanding, with no malicious intent. You are finally permitted to go up to the office of your prospect, but not before your prospective client has been called several times by the security desk, who had indicated that you were insisting that there was a misunderstanding and that you were not leaving. You feel that you were treated discourteously and disrespectfully. You are perturbed and ruminate about the incident as the elevator ascends to the floor where your prospective client awaits your late arrival. You have permitted yourself to be controlled by the situation. You have reacted without thinking. If you had given the situation just three seconds of thought, you likely would have had a calculated and well thought out response.

Here's the question: Are you going to let that isolated incident affect you, possibly influencing the outcome of the meeting, or are you going to let it go? Here is a suggestion for you, only internalize positive ideas and ambitions. Stop letting negative thoughts and frustrations affect you and the outcomes that you seek in your life and business or career. In the scenario described above, you need to be on top of your game and close the deal.

While I understand that it is often difficult for us to let things go when we feel frustrated, we must remain focused on our objectives. We must exercise our will and direct our full attention and resources in the present; so as to avoid diluting our efforts by spending time worrying about things that are now beyond our control. We must always seek to maximize our results. Our will can help us do that.

The third intellectual faculty is our *imagination*. Albert Einstein once said, "Imagination is more important than knowledge." I wholeheartedly agree. Imagination is the creation of everything. Without imagination, nothing happens. We can imagine great things happening to us or we can imagine doom and gloom. We can think about all the positive potential outcomes, or we can literally worry ourselves sick. We can imagine all the things that could go wrong, or we can imagine a life of fulfillment and joy.

You have the ability to imagine your life as beautiful and grand, or you can imagine it as dismal and unsatisfactory. Remember, in our conscious mind, we have the ability to choose and we can choose to imagine anything – even things that don't exist yet in physical form. It's entirely up to you. This is probably one of the most important concepts that I can convey to you between the covers of this book. The direction of your life is solely within your control. Use the extraordinary power of your imagination to create the life that you want to live, and don't hold back. Remember, everything starts with an idea before it is transformed into physical form. Dream big!

The next intellectual faculty is *memory*. We are all born with a phenomenal memory, but it is a matter of how you utilize or exercise it that counts. Memory is something that can even be developed just by incorporating a series of ridiculous association tricks. The point here is that you can remember anything you want to remember. The problem for many of us is that from the time we were children, we may have heard things like, "Oh, Johnny has a terrible memory; he can't remember anything." So we grow up believing just that. What we have been told and what we choose to tell ourselves has an undeniable effect on our lives. You can have a stellar memory but you must choose to exercise it, and use it to benefit you in your daily life.

We say things like, "I can't remember anything. I can't even remember what I had for breakfast yesterday morning, let alone the names of all my clients." What has happened of course, is that we have told our subconscious mind for ten, twenty, thirty, forty, or even fifty years that we have a terrible memory, therefore our subconscious mind gets the message that remembering names or faces isn't important. So what happens? When we walk down the street and we meet someone, the person says, "Hi, my name is Johnny." We respond, "Hello, Johnny. Good to meet you." Thirty seconds later, for the life of us, we can't remember his name. For too many years, we've told our subconscious minds that retaining this information isn't important. So immediately upon hearing a name, the subconscious mind files it in the file labeled "Irrelevant Information" and of course when you need it, it is nearly impossible to retrieve it. The first step to improving your memory is to believe that you are capable of improving it. Once you establish that, you are well on your way, because now the subconscious mind is told that retention and preservation are important. This will support you on your way to improving this faculty.

The next intellectual faculty is our *intuition*. Referring again back to Dr. Wayne Dyer, "If prayer is you talking to God, then intuition is God talking to you." That is a wonderful statement, but there is more to the equation. There is a concern here that I will raise, that is we tend to at times misuse this faculty. In life, we often ask for help and even at times, divine intervention. We ask for guidance or direction from an infinite power. Theology calls it God; science calls it energy, and others may call it the universe. For our purposes, it really doesn't matter what you call it because it doesn't matter who or what you ask, what matters is that you trust your ability to know the right answer when it appears. We may inquire, "Well, I want to know how I can achieve my dreams. How can I get to where I want to be? How do I attract what I want into my life?" When we're presented with these options and challenges, whether from an external source or internally, very typically we ask the wrong questions.

We ask, "Is this right or wrong?" "Should I or shouldn't I?" "How much is it?" When really, the only question that we should be asking is, "If I act on this idea or this information, will it move me in the direction of my goal?" You have to trust your intuition to answer this question for you, and it usually answers with a 'gut' feeling or visceral response. We've all had this experience of just knowing what is right within our own hearts and minds. No one had to tell us, we just knew. This is your intuition, and it can become very powerful if you learn to exercise and use it for good. For example, there are many times during the course of normal life that you will meet someone new. It could be a friend, co-worker, business contact or a random person on the street. When we meet someone, we can usually get a sense of who they are and what they are about in the first few minutes. Now, obviously we don't learn much verbally, but we will likely intuitively know if someone is authentic, or if they are attempting to conceal something or perhaps have an agenda, good or otherwise. We recognize it and the more you trust these responses, the more pronounced they will become. Of course, in order to start recognizing these traits we have to be engaged and awake. We need to begin to understand people and how they operate.

Now once you get a nudge from your intuition about what action to take or who to trust, act immediately. Don't wait for circumstances to change. Don't wait until its perfect. Circumstances will never be perfect. Action should always take the lead over perfection. The quality of the questions that we ask will give us the answers we need, if we know how to listen.

Your question may also take this form: "Is this idea in harmony with my purpose, my vision, and my goals?" Again, if the answer is yes, then take action. You do not need to know exactly how you are going to do everything before you get started. The *how* shouldn't matter at this point. The Wright brothers didn't know how they were going to introduce us to the idea of flying. Thomas Edison didn't know how he was going to illuminate the world with the light bulb. Bill Gates didn't know how he was going to put a computer on the desk of every person in America.

What mattered to them was the why. As they began to focus and become emotionally involved with their ideas, as they let their intuition guide them through the process, the desire was inside them to attract ideas from an unseen power. They acted on those ideas as long as such actions and ideas moved them in the direction of their objectives.

The last intellectual faculty is *reason*. This is what separates human beings from animals. This is our ability to choose. This is the God-like part of us. We have the ability to reason inductively or deductively. We can either gather independent facts and create our own conclusions, or we can approach things from the reverse angle, starting with a conclusion and then investigating to find the facts that support our conclusion or theory.

This allows us to look at all sides in exploring what we want. It is the ability to reason effectively that will assist you in navigating any perceived barriers that may show up on your journey. What is vitally important is that you take action, no matter how insignificant it may seem, in relation to your goals.

Refuse the ideas that that will prevent you from getting started, and take the first step.

Of course, just as some of our other faculties, reason can be used as a negative or positive attribute depending how you choose to exercise it. You can assure yourself that you will conquer the world, or you can do the easy sell on yourself and not even unbuckle the sofa seatbelt – you make the call.

By appropriately employing all of our intellectual faculties and blending them with our renewed thought process, we not only gain control over what we are thinking in our conscious mind, but we gain control over our emotional mind, which of course is our subconscious mind. This immediately allows us to dramatically alter the action we are taking, thus delivering improved results.

If you are steadfastly focused on your goals or objectives, and you are determined to obtain and or attain these goals, you will experience success. Whether it's money, a new job, true love, or great health, you're going to create those results in your life based on how you think and what action steps you take. Again, the image we focus on is going to dictate our results. But you must act. You cannot sit around and wait for things to happen. Don't expect to be successful if all you do is think about it but never get off your sofa. Wishing and hoping is not the path to fulfillment or success, just as the lottery is not a solid retirement plan.

Now that you have a broader understanding of how the mind functions and how powerful it really is, the next step in the process is to raise the awareness of what is possible. There are many who get to this stage of their life-development, but they stop short because internally they are overwhelmed with uncertainty and skepticism. In order for you to scale incredible heights, you must understand that anything is possible and that you can achieve it. There is one single common thread among all great achievers, and that is the belief within each of them as they pursued their dreams and broke new ground. It is an idea that is so simple to understand and so integral to every wonderful accomplishment, yet it is one that most people fail to recognize to their own detriment. You must believe in yourself and your abilities, no matter what.

There is additional information on our website at www. changeyourresults.com.

CHAPTER 4
THE POWER OF YOU

You need to overcome the tug of people against you as you reach for high goals.
George S. Patton

• We are not taught to think effectively to get good results – it is a learned skill.

• We choose what thoughts occupy our minds and those thoughts determine our results.

• Our conscious mind is our 'thinking' mind and our subconscious mind is our 'feeling' mind.

• The Intellectual Faculties are like our mind's muscles and if not exercised, we never reach our full potential.

• The most successful people in history had an unwavering belief in self.

CHAPTER 5

YES YOU CAN

It's always too early to quit.
Norman Vincent Peale

We hear the phrase 'believe in yourself' frequently. It sounds easy, but if you don't believe in yourself it can seem like climbing a glacier. Yet you must realize that you are endowed with unique talents and abilities. No this isn't just in theory! We each have very different capacities for imagination and creation, therefore we each have the potential to change our own lives, and the lives of others if we choose. It is this fundamental truth that will guide you every step of the way in pursuit of the life of your dreams. You first must realize that you absolutely have the capacity to achieve your dreams – even if you think there is evidence to the contrary! Even if you've never achieved great things so far, that does not mean you can't start right now.

In the previous chapter we talked about how your mind works and how you can choose to harness its incredible power and exercise the skills necessary to improve your results. It is for these reasons that you cannot write yourself off or assume you have gone as far as you can go. Not that many people don't try, but it's just a cop out. Many people assume that in order to change their lives they will have to work at it, and the bottom line is they just don't want to. They are comfortable where they are, or so they believe. The problem is that nothing ever stays the same, we are all in constant motion and the world is in a state of continual change. If we get comfortable where we are and refuse to change, we are quickly left behind. Change is constant, ultimately your success is entirely dependent on the conscious decisions that you make minute by minute.

There should be no doubt in your mind as to what you are capable of accomplishing. Sure you will have questions about exactly how you will reach your destination. Most will feel that this is natural, and for most of us, it is. It may also be good to note that this thought process is likely the result of one of our paradigms. Everyone who has ever achieved anything great in their lives was, at one point, faced with uncertainty about how they were going to realize their dream. But there was also another common element in these individuals: they all believed that they had the capacity to pull it off so they kept searching for answers and persisted notwithstanding what may have seemed like insurmountable odds.

Belief in self is essential, but ironically many of us lack this as a result of our belief system. As we already pointed out, from a very early age we listen far too much to outside sources, letting them define for us what we can or cannot do. The reality is that some of us allow other people to control who we are. In fact, just last night I was with a group of people who demonstrated this concept in action. I had mentioned to them some time ago that I was planning to write a book. To some people this is still a big joke as I didn't strike them as the type to sit down and put my thoughts on paper. They were absolutely convinced that I would not be able to do it. I suppose that the fact that you are now reading these words is confirmation they were mistaken. But at the time I was challenged with comments such as "Writing a book? Who do you think you are? The next J. K. Rowling? Are you crazy? Have you lost your marbles? What gives you the authority? You're an expert in what?" It would give any logical person pause, and it did me too, but only for a brief moment. I knew that through my experiences, study and knowledge I could offer help, and direction to those who would accept it.

However, that negative attitude is exactly what prevents countless people from living great lives. Not all, but many. In fact, comments like those are often significant enough to stop someone from pursuing a goal before they even get started. That's why, no matter what it is— progressing in business, starting a new business, developing relationships, or yes writing a book—you need to know that it can be done and that you can do it. You must recognize your own unlimited potential and fulfill it. You must believe in yourself even if no one else agrees with you at the time. Eventually they will see your achievements and hopefully want to know how you did it, so that they may emulate your results.

I have a friend who used to be rather shy, we'd be out enjoying ourselves someplace with friends and he'd say, "I think I'm going to go over and talk to that girl." Rather than support his decision, many people in the group would try to keep him locked into his timid state. They would say things like, "She'll never be interested in you. Why waste your time? She's out of your league." This is precisely what is wrong with our view of ourselves, we believe what everyone else thinks, not what we know to be true. This poor guy was trying to break out of his shell, kick through the terror barrier but was being continually dragged back under by people, who for whatever reason (perhaps to protect their own lack of self-confidence), would go out of their way to keep him pinned down.

Understand that when you move forward, you push into new territory and achieve lofty goals, there will be detractors. Some will be jealous and assume by default that if you are moving ahead they are falling behind, and no one likes to fall behind. They may also honestly be trying to protect you – sometimes the people closest to you will fall in this category. They are afraid you will fail and they don't want you to be hurt. Because they don't see you as a high achiever, they assume the worst but in reality their opinions don't matter. What matters is that you believe you can achieve, and then take the steps to make it so.

Most of the time we don't realize that we tend to build our lives based on what other people say. You are doing yourself an extreme disservice by letting other opinions be the dominating force behind your own self-assessment, and in turn your progress. There are always going to be detractors who, because of their own fears, seek to reinforce their beliefs by putting limits on others. Whether consciously or unconsciously, these people restrict those around them in order to feel better about themselves. That's why, as pointed out in the first chapter, you must be aware and vigilant about who you spend your time with. I'm very careful with decisions I make with regard to my circle of influence, because the group of friends, family, and associates I spend a lot of time with is going to make an immense difference in my life. By practicing the same thing it will make a big difference in yours as well.

Yes, this may mean you have to limit the time that you spend with some of the people in your life. We're not talking about abandoning your family or friends, but we are talking about ensuring you are moving in the direction of your goals with the fewest impediments. This is necessary, at least until you are strong enough to withstand the negativity without it affecting you and your ambitions.

While this may be somewhat simple with friends or co-workers, family can be complicated. You can on a temporary basis limit your time with those family members who are the most destructive, until you are able to effectively deal with their pessimistic outlook. I also strongly recommend that you actively seek out new friendships with the type of people you want to associate with. These may be successful entrepreneurs, positive and supportive people, or those who offer encouragement and real solutions. Change can be viewed as challenging, and having someone or even a group of people that can be in your corner and encourage you is very important to your ongoing success. You're going to gravitate toward them and they're going to gravitate toward you, as you change the way you think and the way you act. You're in harmony with them, and they are in harmony with you – much more so than the others who would want to tear you down or see you fail.

If they are the type of people who are always endeavoring to expand, always striving to go that extra step, always making that extra effort to grow, then you are going to emulate their actions and way of thinking. If they are not, if they are the type of people who are always looking for the short cut or the easy way out, then you will likely fall into the same trap. You will restrict yourself. Having a trusted sphere of advisors that keep you aware of possibilities and reality, is a good thing. It's important to have discussions and talk things through. You don't want to surround yourself with negative energy that comes from fear or lack of understanding. You don't want to get caught up in a group of people who are always saying, "You can't do that. You don't have that ability." That sort of thing seeps into your subconscious mind and prevents you from ever attempting something new. It prevents you from exploring and discovering the joy that lies in unknown territory.

Just this past week, I had someone come to me and demonstrate this principle. I was speaking with a gentleman that works for a family member about seizing on a particular business opportunity, when he said, "I'm not a business person like you. I can't do this." Well, says who?!!

I wasn't a business person either at first. I worked for somebody else for many, many years. That didn't stop me from surging ahead in pursuit of a dream. I learned, made my share of mistakes, and then learned some more. Over time, I was able to become successful. I was able to become a knowledgeable and progressive businessman.

Once we change our mindset, once we believe in ourselves, then the awareness of our unlimited potential will grow. When we are able to understand that we have the ability to do anything that we can possibly dream, then we are already on the road to success.

As one of my mentors, Bob Proctor, rightly points out, you already have the ability, you already have the potential. You were born with it. You were born with all the tools you need to live a prosperous and fulfilling life.

When I work either one-on-one or in a group setting, I show these amazing and wonderful individuals how to use the tools with which you have been gifted and blessed. We show you how to expand on them, how to really make that difference in your life. You can achieve anything that you truly desire! You may just need that little bit of extra guidance to assist you on the road to possibility.

Terror Barrier

While you certainly have the inherent capacity to achieve anything that you desire, you will have to work for it. You will encounter challenges. It will require tremendous effort and you will be forced to get outside of your comfort zone. One of the biggest hindrances to progress in life—whether you are talking about achieving goals in your professional or personal life—is the fact that you have experienced fear. In your dealings with your employer or your clients as well as your relationship with your family, fear is a constant factor.

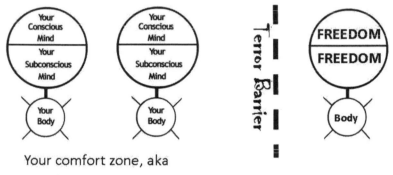

Your comfort zone, aka your box.

Although fear is considered natural, it is in reality not natural, as a matter of fact it is something that we are taught. Let me be clear, there are situations where fear is a necessity. For example, we teach our children not to jump out of a moving car, to do this we instill fear as a tool. This is very simply fear of what the outcome would likely be. In other words, the experts tell us that some level of fear is a good thing. This is however not the case when it comes to the big picture goals for your life. There have been ideas floated, that fear is a motivator. This is not the case. Fear is debilitating and will, if you permit it to, hold you back from seeking and realizing your dreams. Choose not to allow fear to be an impediment in your motivation to seek and achieve.

It's important to understand that the emotion of fear exists nowhere, except in your mind. Therefore our fears are typically based on information that we've been preprogrammed with, accepted uncritically from an outside source or that we may have developed out of some irrational associations or prior conditioning. In other words, we have been taught, among other emotions, to be fearful. Now there are some natural fears that are instinctive and I'm not talking about those. Of course, if a lion is chasing you in the jungle you are going to be fearful and this fear will likely assist in your escape. The type of fear I'm talking about is what we feel when not in mortal danger. For example, the kind of fear you have when you think you may lose your job, or when a loved one is ill, or perhaps when you have to speak in front of a large audience. None of these put us in mortal danger, yet they can cause great fear and anxiety, if we allow it.

For example, I've asked many clients and students a very direct question: "How much money do you make in a year?" And they've said to me, for example, "Well, I make $40,000 per year." I would argue the reason they are not making more is because they don't believe they can. When I explain that they can absolutely make more money, the first question they ask is "How?" They've already been through this ritual in their own mind and they can't seem to get past this point. As soon as they don't know *how*, they retreat. They are butting up against what we call the terror barrier. Their fear has blinded them to the truth. Their reasoning is, "If I don't know how I am going to do something then it must be impossible." This is, of course nonsense, and in most cases just an excuse. Their thinking, while effective in keeping them in their comfort zone, is flawed because it keeps them from achieving more. It tells them, "There is a risk here, and I know I don't want to take a risk. If I don't take a risk I don't have to risk failure." That is certainly true, but it's also true that if you never take a risk then you're never going to actually achieve anything additional in life. Isn't that the real failure?

This type of fear is why you see people working at the same job from the time they get out of high school all the way through to retirement. Within a year or two of retirement, many people find that they don't even get to enjoy their additional time and freedom. They scrimp their entire lives, never getting to enjoy life and then they retire and do the same thing. They have been so rigidly programmed, so conservative, for their entire lives, that they are unable to break that pattern. Instead of taking that extra step toward a deep-seated goal, they remain passive and watch opportunities pass them by. When they contemplate something more, they are stricken with an overriding sense of fear and stay affixed within their comfort zone.

Maybe they wanted to do something grand, but now it's too late. Maybe they let themselves get kicked around, and wish they had stood up for themselves. Is that the kind of life you want? Perhaps, when faced with a challenge, a set back or a situation that you first interpret as negative, you need to take a moment and put things in perspective. If you are faced with the possibility of a layoff, you could consider the idea that this could be the opportunity that you have been waiting for. It's all a matter of perception. We can look at a situation and say, "That's it, it's all over. I'm going to lose the house, the car, the boat, everything." Or, you can look at the same situation and say, "Maybe this is the kick in the backside I needed to actually start the business that I have been thinking and talking about for the last twenty years." Regrets can be very hard to live with, and while you need to make educated decisions and mitigate uncalculated risk, no one wants to cheat themselves out of the life they should've had.

You can do whatever it is you truly desire, and while it is true you have been conditioned to stay in one comfort zone your whole life, no one is forcing you to stay there. Unfortunately, too many people fail to realize this fundamental truth: We are the only ones that restrict ourselves, nobody else can do it for us. You choose to allow these thoughts and ideas that have been passed down from others to dictate your life, but you are still responsible to choose that same old path each and every day. By the same token, we're the only ones that can change ourselves. Nobody else can do that for you either. So many of people are looking for the "easy" button, for the easy way to get what they think that they want. This is where those that are serious make positive progress, and those that are looking for the quick fix or the success pill become separated. My friends, there are no quick fixes, or happy pills and you definitely cannot write a check and expect positive change. Achieving your goals will involve dedication, money, persistence, smart work, time and a coach. If you have and understand at least a portion of what it will take to make your goals a reality, you've already made significant progress.

I have seen some decide to change their lives and become successful, but then they set about cheating and belittling people in their efforts to get to the top. Understand that you don't have to step all over people or become someone that you are not. You cannot and will not win in the long term if you're always competing. Many of us have been raised that we must compete and beat the other guy to win – but that's not true. There is a place for everyone, and each of us has a different purpose, so it isn't necessary to run over anyone else or destroy what they are building. All you can and should do is focus on what you want to do.

You are not able to predict what someone else may say or do. You cannot change the actions that others may take, but you can change what you do and how you do it. Don't get caught up in the habit of trying to tear other people down so that you can prop yourself up. Life doesn't work that way. There is no shortage of success to be had in this world. You do not have to steal it from anyone else in order for you to obtain it. Concentrate your efforts on yourself and overcoming your own fears, for that is worthy of your effort.

By merely understanding that the terror barrier exists, you can kick through it. You must also understand that unless you are actually challenging your fears on a regular basis, you are not growing. You shouldn't expect everything to happen overnight. Success is a process and there is a cycle in life. In order to succeed you need to be constantly striving for growth. Those people who are diligent in gaining information and in expanding their awareness, are the ones who truly succeed in life. Those that laugh at others who study, read books, and actually seek information are the ones, in most cases, who are going to be relegated to mediocre jobs they don't really like for the rest of their lives. They are the ones who are not really going to be able to expand and achieve what it is they desire.

They see the car, they see the house, they see something that they want, and that's as far as it goes. They think, "Oh, I wish I could have that. But I'm not rich. Someday, maybe." They deflate their ambitions and chalk up the success of others to a natural ability, luck or a rich uncle that they just don't have themselves. They say, "I would love to have my own business, but I can't do that. I don't know how to run a company." They say these things instead of turning the situation around and saying, "You know what? I can do anything I want. Sure, I'm going to have to get some additional information, and maybe I will have to get a business coach or a consultant, but I can do this. Maybe I have to take a course, go back to school, or obtain additional and specialized knowledge, but I will do whatever it is I need to do." Or, "That's the car that I'm going to buy. That's the home that I'm going to buy." It's all in the approach and perception that makes something achievable or not.

What we need to understand is that kicking through that terror barrier is a liberating feeling – in fact just getting beyond the fear can feel better than perhaps anything that you may have experienced in the past. Know that expanding your horizons, expanding your knowledge, and experiencing new things is the way to reach your goals and set even higher and bigger ones.

Once we have that knowledge and that awareness, things tend to become much easier. This is because once you have conquered some of the small fears that are standing in your way, you then have the confidence and courage to tackle what you perceived as big ones.

If you already know how to do something, it's not much of a challenge. It's not a goal. It's not true growth. It's those things that we don't know how to do that constitute progress. Once you create a situation conducive to growth, you are really moving toward your goal; once you are moving toward your goal, then you are increasing the strength, will, and awareness to keep right on going. You can then build upon that even further. If you want that house overlooking the ocean, or maybe you want one on the ocean, you must first understand that you have the potential and capability to reach that goal and make it a reality.

I work with some individuals in "The Power of A" – Strategic Accountability coaching program, and we'll typically get six weeks into the program and I'll usually have 75-80% of the participants say to me, "Shawn, how come you didn't tell me this six weeks ago?" I'll look at them and say, "Well, I did." This is true! It's just that at that point in time, six weeks prior, they didn't have that awareness or that knowledge base to fully grasp what I was talking about. I outlined the principles, but they didn't really hear them because they weren't ready. But once they gain that awareness, all of the sudden it's like somebody flips a light switch and they say, "Oh my goodness. This makes so much sense. This is real. I never understood this before."

The same is true with business or personal opportunities that come along. Because your fears are inhibiting what you can see in your everyday life, opportunities pass you by each and every day. Often, once someone has started growing and pursuing their dreams, it will seem as if their lives suddenly come together and opportunities are springing up everywhere like magic! It's not magic – the truth is those opportunities were always there but they didn't have the awareness to see them and take advantage of them. It can be a little sobering to think that everything you ever wanted in your life is a mere arm's length away, but you just don't have the awareness to push beyond your fear and reach out and grab it.

Once you understand, once you kick through that terror barrier, that fake brick wall, on the other side is freedom. That keeps expanding, getting easier every time you do it. The first time I stood in front of a group of people to give a presentation, which was many years ago, my heart was in my throat. I probably stood up there for a good thirty or forty seconds before I spoke one word. Obviously, it's a little different today as I've done it many, many times, but the point is that the more you do it, the easier it becomes. The same thing applies to any aspect of your life that you find challenging. I know people that can't sleep for a week before having to stand up in front of a group of their peers because they are so nervous about having to give a ten-minute presentation. Every time you kick through the terror barrier, it doesn't matter what it is, it will become less painful. Maybe it's driving, maybe it's flying, maybe it's taking that step toward a new, and what may appear as challenging goal. Maybe it's the risk of quitting that job you hate and going out on your own, despite the perceived security that comes with your current position (keep in mind that job security is not real, especially today). Maybe it's actually starting that new business, or finding true love. If you remain afraid to venture out into the unknown, if you are unwilling to do the necessary hard work that is required in any worthwhile endeavor, then you're never going to actually achieve what it is you truly desire. I don't care what that is, it can be great wealth or great health, if you are not going to do anything about it, you are not going to obtain it. You need to invoke the Law of Action in order to achieve what it is you truly want. You have to make the effort. You HAVE make a decision to be ACCOUNTABLE.

If you are strong enough to maintain that image of what you want on the screen of your mind, to hold it to the exclusion of all outside distractions, then you have the potential to achieve your dreams. Remember, everything you see around you, no matter what it is, was at one time an idea in somebody's mind that moved into physical form. Was there some action required? Absolutely. It was still just an idea. Whether it's the Taj Mahal, the CN Tower or a new Lexus, it makes no difference. It was just an idea in somebody's mind at some point that we can now experience as reality. You can make your ideas happen just the same, as long as you understand that you have the potential to do that, as long as you believe in yourself and take action.

You have to understand that you already have the potential, it's not something you have to find. You have the ability as well, even if you've never used that ability to this point. Now you will have the tools through this book to start on your own path to growth and success. All you need to do is utilize those tools. Everything starts with recognizing that you are capable of extraordinary achievements. You must commit to overcome your fears and strive to obtain that which your heart most vehemently desires.

We all have a comfort zone and too often, we don't want to leave that place of perceived security. You get an idea, maybe even start to execute it, and come up against those old fears – your own terror barrier - and that threshold keeps you in a state of superficial safety and unhappiness. It exists for all of us. The problem is that far too many people turn around at this point and wind up right back in their comfort zone. In order to grow, we have to break through.

Our natural tendency is to want to stay within our box, our safe haven. But the path to achieving success is printed on the outside of the box. Unless we abandon the box, we are never going to be able to achieve our goals or reach our desired destination.

For many people, even a painful and appalling situation is still at times much more comfortable than the unknown. They may convince themselves, "Sure this situation is far from ideal, but at least I *know* this pain and sense of unrest and that has to be better than not knowing." This mindset will confine you to a life that never even comes close to contentment let alone reaching the ballpark of happiness. Once you are able to venture outside of what you have always known, you will open yourself up to a whole new world of possibilities. You must first summon the fundamental strength necessary to cross the threshold and take those first bold steps, increasing your confidence that you will be able to do it again and again.

CHAPTER 5
YES YOU CAN

A successful man is one who can lay a firm foundation with the bricks others have thrown at him.
David Brinkley

• We are all products of our beliefs. Don't allow outside sources to mold your beliefs.

• You must choose; your comfort zone, or progress. Only you can create your own destiny.

• Fear does not exist outside our own minds.

• Fear must be eliminated in order to gain the confidence to move on.

• As you overcome small fears and meet with some success it will give you the courage to tackle the big fears that are holding you back.

CHAPTER 6

WHAT DO YOU REALLY WANT?

The person who gets the farthest is generally the one who is willing to do and dare. The sure-thing boat never gets far from shore.
Dale Carnegie

There are a great number of people who are unhappy in this world—far too many people in my opinion. While many individuals are simply suffering from a general feeling of unease, uncomfortable in their own skin, others have a vast array of reasons as to why they are unhappy. In fact, if you ask them what is wrong, they will quickly be able to break into a whole litany of things that they don't like about their life and their current situation. Yet if you then ask these same individuals what would make them happy, they seem to struggle to come up with much. If you were to ask the same people for solutions to their various problems they become conspicuously quiet. If you press further and inquire as to what would present them with even a modest level of satisfaction, you will be met with a flurry of "ums" and "ahs" that fall between a whole lot of silence. In short, it would appear that they have no clue what they really want.

This is a very unfortunate reality for more people than you might guess. I present this information not to disparage those that may be struggling to find themselves, but to illustrate the point that not having any idea of what you want is the root cause of much despair in people's lives. It is a genuine source of frustration. I am not suggesting this is an easy thing to do, to figure out what would make your life great; it can be a quite a challenge for some. Think about it. Can you answer the question? What do you really want? If you can't answer right this second, don't feel bad. As we pointed out, you are certainly not alone. What's interesting is the fact that even though this question often goes unanswered, it is probably one of the most important questions that you can ever ask yourself. It defines everything that you are, and everything that you want to become. How can you possibly know what to do with your life if you have no clue where you are going? It is an extremely powerful question to ponder.

When we think about what will make us happy, we typically tend to focus on superficial things that we are inundated with through media and other sources, on a daily basis. We are flooded with a staggering amount of shiny new material items to entice us. As a result, we often go through life and say, "I want a new home" or "I want a new car." What is it that you really and truly want out of life? Deep down in your soul, what will bring you true happiness? Before you venture off in search of a better life, it is vital that you are able to answer this one simple question. *What do you really want?*

Now don't get me wrong, there is nothing inherently wrong with being drawn to material items. For example, there is nothing wrong with wanting a new car. These items should be looked at as just a piece of the larger puzzle. When we pose the question, what do you really want, we are talking about something larger. We are talking about the entire picture - your deepest desires in life. Those things that delve into your reason for being.

Material items can sometimes be a part of the equation, and can, indeed, give you significant pleasure, but the point of this chapter is larger than that. The point of this chapter is that once you understand what you truly desire in life, you can then set the corresponding goals that will take you where you want to go. There is an honest simplicity about it. If you are unable to answer the fundamental question of what you want, you will surely find yourself wandering aimlessly through life. You will find yourself thinking back on days gone by, wondering why you were unable to make any progress or contemplating why you lost ground from the heights of your success. The answer is simple: You must determine what you want and then go after it.

I put this question to my coaching clients and students and many of them simply have no idea how to answer it. Again this is extremely common, but it is still somewhat surprising when you consider the power that lies in the answer. When I ask my clients what they really want, they often look at me and reluctantly say, "Well, I don't know what I want, Shawn. I just know that I'm not happy. I know that I want more from life."

I try again, pressing a little harder: "C'mon, give it some thought. What do you really want from life?"

Again comes the same answer, "I just don't know. I just know that there is more out there for me."

This is a big problem for a lot of people. They have never really put in the time to discover their fundamental desires.

These are not just people that are struggling financially, or people that find themselves stuck in dead-end jobs. These are people that represent the whole spectrum of individuals, including those who have already been relatively successful in their lives. In fact, many people that enjoy great success in the conventional sense are not really enjoying their lives at all. They still feel that something significant is missing in their lives, that there is a deficiency. They are generally happy with how things are going but they know something is missing. Whether it comes down to aspects of family or just a nagging sense that their lives lack fulfillment, the fact remains that many people are simply struggling with their current state of affairs, all the while they still don't know what they want.

Our coaching programs are specifically designed to help draw out your inner most desires so that you are able to put yourself on track toward a more fulfilling life. It often takes a great deal of conversation, introspection and reflection, but figuring out what you really want is the key to experiencing fulfillment in every aspect of your life. This is because everything else is interconnected with it. You must sufficiently tap into your desires in order to find the path in life that is right for you. Not only that, but you will be much more prone to put forth the extraordinary effort required to achieve your goals if you feel that you are headed in the right direction. This gives your life meaning and adds excitement and passion to your efforts, and will work wonders for your overall attitude and enjoyment.

Think of it like this: Have you ever experienced the thrill of being involved in an activity that truly excited you? It could be anything, it does not matter what it is. For example, if you love to go canoeing, is it a chore for you to plan a trip and prepare yourself for the excursion? Of course not. You excitedly do your research to find the perfect location.

You go to the outdoor store and buy everything that you will need. The night before you are to head out with your friends or family, you get all your gear together, put the canoe up on your vehicle and anticipate the big trip – in fact you may not sleep at all, out of pure anticipation. When the morning arrives, you likely spring out of bed, maybe even before the alarm goes off. Why is that? Because you are excited, because you can't wait to get started, and because you know where you are going and its somewhere you want to be.

Contrast that with a situation where you have to go to work and give a presentation. You dread preparing for it. You reluctantly perform your research and assemble your data. You may stay up all night because you are trying to delay the inevitable which is to happen the next morning. When the alarm goes off, you feel exhausted. You can hardly pry yourself from the covers and roll out of bed. The morning seems much colder and darker than usual. What's the difference between the two scenarios? You got the same amount of sleep as you did before the canoeing trip. Why do you feel so tired before your presentation, so down and out? Well, the answer is quite obvious. If you are unhappy, or if you don't feel a sense of passion behind any given endeavor, then you will likely find yourself suffering from a tremendous lack of motivation.

Here's another example: Let's say that you are a senior vice president in a multi-national corporation. Let's also say that you really value your independence and have a strong desire for autonomy, you love being able to come and go as you please. Do you really think you are going to be happy at a job that requires you to promptly report to an office for ten hours per day so that you can manage all of your employees along with the daily operations? How about if you value spending time with your family, really enjoy volunteering and staying involved in the local community? How satisfied would you be with a job that requires you to be traveling out of town six months out of the year—no matter how much you were paid or how prestigious your job title was? What if holidays were important to you, would you really fare well in a job where you were made to feel guilty about taking time away from work—even if you had four weeks of guaranteed vacation?

Now contrast that with a job that allows you tremendous flexibility in creating your own schedule, is in a field that calls upon you to find ways of improving the community by focusing on neighborhood projects, and encourages you to take time off to recharge your batteries. Do you think you would be more motivated to get your job done? You bet you would. If you discovered the kind of job that you truly wanted, you might even find yourself in a position where you would look forward to getting out of bed in the morning and going to work…gasp! Is that really possible? Of course it is.

The above example may or may not resonate with you. Let me ask you another question: What if you could start and develop a business that would allow you the freedom to spend time with your family and friends, of course assisting others or volunteering as well? What if you so enjoyed your business that getting up in the morning was the best time of your day? What if you structured your business so that it generated enough money for everything you wanted and needed? Does this sound too good to be true? Here is what I know with certainty, the above is not too good to be true and if you want it and are willing to commit to what it takes, it can be yours. I've watched countless people, just like you achieve financial independence, I've witnessed numerous companies of all sizes increase profitability even through troubled economic times. Every individual and organization was proactive, they engaged a coach or consultant. It's possible, you just have to be ready for change and want it bad enough.

It all comes down to discovering what you really want out of life. Everyone is put on this earth with a unique set of skills, abilities, and talents. What are yours? How would you like to use them? Why are you here? It is up to you to spend a sufficient amount of time examining those questions. You must take the time to fully understand your talents and utilize them to help you lead a satisfying life, and make the most of your gifts. It is up to you to determine your purpose in life and develop a plan to make it happen. As we discussed, accountability and action are the keys.

This is not intended to weigh you down in a heavy discussion. We all have different views and this is not to pretend that there is only one correct way to go through life. That is a decision that only you can make. It is certainly important to identify those things that are most valuable to you and recognize your underlying reasons for taking action. Understanding those reasons, at your core, will provide the much needed energy to carry forward when you encounter challenges or perhaps even fail. Yes, you will face challenges and maybe even experience failure at some point. You see, although we may anticipate that the process will be easy, once we know our direction of travel, this is not always the case. Things will likely work at a quicker pace perhaps even a little smoother, but please know that there will always be things that will need to be worked through and around. As a side note, failure is something that all of us face from time to time, this doesn't mean that it's all over, failures are very simply put, learning experiences.

Living a fulfilling life does not mean living a life that is free from concerns or challenges. I am not implying that once you decide what you want, you will never have to be concerned about anything. This is often what prevents people from taking any steps toward a goal. They feel that things will just occur on their own. That if the right idea had come along, then they would already be living a wonderful life, but this is not how it works. It is a mistake for people to think this way although many still do. They see the success of others and immediately infer that those people are just naturally gifted, that things just fell into their laps. Nothing could be further from the truth.

The reality is that once you discover what you want, you still have a great deal of work to do. You will forge ahead with a new-found determination and persistence. You won't let anything stand in your way. That is the real secret. It all comes from knowing what you want to spend your life pursuing. When you know what you want, you are still responsible for your utilizing the gifts that you have been given and taking action to achieve it. Yet again, accountability is key.

That is the second part of the equation. Once you discover what you want, you must be willing to enact a plan to make it happen. It's not enough just to know where you want to go. You have to be willing to develop the plan to get there. There are those that have no idea what they want, have no plan and are typically unhappy.

Then there are those that know what they want, but are still unwilling to go get it. They are perhaps even more unhappy because they have identified what they want and they believe that it lies out of their reach, taunting them on a daily basis. Referring back to the previous example, if you happen to know that you enjoy working in your community, and you are in a position that prevents you from ever feeling that sense of contribution, then can you truly be happy? Can you ever truly consider yourself successful?

What is Success?

When you sit down and think about what you want, you first have to know what success means. Earl Nightingale defined success this way, "Success is the progressive realization of a worthy ideal." Let's take a look at his definition for a moment. He is saying that we should always be moving in the direction of our valuable and defined goal (our success). Change is constant and we can never say that "we have arrived." We are continuously attaining success. An ideal has been described as an idea that you've fallen in love with. Therefore, your ideal is going to be different from anyone else's, and as long it motivates you, it is worthwhile. It should be said then that, achieving our success is a constant and ongoing process, one which we have to be committed to.

I often find that some people who are feeling that something is missing, have been caught up in the expectations of others. Perhaps they went to school to become a professional, such as a doctor or lawyer, and maybe even knew part way through that was not what they wanted. But, they didn't make a decision to do what they truly wanted to do. They were instead, more concerned about disappointing people who may have been supporting them, that they ended up in a career they didn't really like, and as a result were exceptionally unhappy. Now is the time for introspection. Think about what really makes you happy because that is where your ultimate success will come from.

I would like to then alter the success question a bit and ask not just what success *means* to you, but what it is *worth* to you? This gives it some added perspective. It is a way of assigning a measure of effort and sacrifice to the ideas you created, to your ideals.

So, once you have defined your idea of success, take a moment and think about that question, right now - What is success worth to you? How different would your life be, if you took the requisite action to go after your true idea of success, and then ultimately achieved your goal? What is the value that you would place upon adapting to the lifestyle that you have always dreamed of? How much is it worth to you to be able to live a life of fulfillment? What would you be willing to do in order to get it? What would you be willing to sacrifice? What would you be willing to give up? Time with family and friends? Money? These are questions that help you really drill down and get to the heart of what you really want, and how committed you are to your success.

People sometimes say to me, "Shawn, you know I'd really like to come to your seminars or join your membership program, but I just can't afford to do it." And I ask, "Well, why is that?"

"Because of the cost." Is the typical response.

Now I love what I do, and I consider it part of my purpose to do it. At the same time, I will tell you that I need to ensure that I am moving ahead as well. At the same time, I also realize that each person's financial situation is different. Not being able to afford a seminar or coaching is a valid argument. Having said that, let me ask you something: if you came away from my seminar, or from anybody else's for that matter (there are a lot of great coaches and teachers), with one idea that catapulted you in the direction of your goal and significantly shortened your learning curve, what do you suppose that would be worth to you? Would you consider it a great investment in yourself?

When you evaluate your options, you must always give proper consideration to what it means to your future.

Investing in yourself is a necessity, you should therefore never feel guilty about it. You should always focus on the end result, that tidbit of information that will catapult you in the direction of your goal. So what would it be worth to you if you received a piece of information that put you on track toward your goal and shortened your learning curve tremendously? The true answer to that question, of course, is that it would be inestimable. We should all be involved in a constant search for new information that will better our lives and that will ultimately make us more successful. You can not put a monetary amount on true success. So you have to know what you want and determine what it is worth to you.

Even the best athletes, companies, and leaders are continuously making efforts to improve themselves. If they are not, they are not likely to occupy the top spot for very long. There is always someone else out there who is willing to put in the required extra effort. There is always someone else who will set the bar even higher. This speaks to the point I made earlier. Many people get caught in the trap of believing that successful people are just going through the motions based on their natural abilities and good fortune. While I don't want to take anything away from those that are naturally gifted in any particular area, I would be willing to gamble that in most cases, if you go behind the scenes, you will discover a great deal of hard work, determination and persistence. It should also not come as a shock to you to learn that the top people in their fields also happen to love what they do. They have been able to identify it and go get it. Many of these people have worked for decades until they became an 'overnight sensation' and known to the rest of us. Are you willing to do the same thing? Are prepared to do what it takes, notwithstanding the sacrifices?

It all goes back to the same overriding question. What do you really want? You need to be able to very clearly and succinctly determine the answer. It's not enough just to say, "I want true love." Well, what does that mean to you? Companionship, marriage, a family? What is it worth to you? To use a couple of material examples, you can't just say, "I want money." You can't just say, "I want a new boat." Why do you want those things? What are they worth to you? You have to be specific. You have to say, "I am purchasing a brand new fully-loaded; red, white, and black, Chris-Craft Launch 22 by a specific date. In order to do that, I must raise my income by $6,000 per month over the course of the next 18 months." That will give you a much better idea of what is really involved, and help you focus on the steps that will make it happen. Do you see the difference?

Keep in mind our example of the top performers in their fields. Ask any of them what they want and they will be able to give you a specific answer. They will be able to go into great detail about what they want and what they expect from themselves in both the near-and-long-term. They have taken the time to give it careful consideration and as a result, they increase their chances of getting it dramatically. This is certainly not any great revelation, but nevertheless, we all need a reminder once in a while as to the effectiveness of this technique—myself included.

You must have a really clear picture that you can hold on the screen of your mind to the exclusion of all outside distractions. In order for us to truly have what it is we want in our lives, in order for us to truly achieve what it is we desire, we need to know exactly what we want. I think you'll agree with me that if you don't have a clear picture, you're going to be confused as to the course of action you need to take. This will result in anxiety which is not an emotional response conducive to achieving the life that you truly desire. Anxiety and fear, while perceived as natural emotions, will not keep you in a state of mind that will help you move in a positive direction. A small measure of fear (respect) can help keep you sharp, but too much of it can be debilitating and extremely counterproductive. So clearly define what you want and stay focused on the big picture. Don't allow negative emotions or people to interfere with your journey of achievement.

Understand that if you focus on the big picture, the smaller goals are going to start falling into place. It will take effort, but you will see them start to align over a relatively short time. So, don't worry so much about where those next few dollars are going to come from. If you are focused on your ultimate goal, move forward by conquering your fears, then the smaller goals along the way will begin to take shape. I assure you that your results will be extraordinary.

CHAPTER 6
WHAT DO YOU REALLY WANT?

Man never made any material as resilient as the human spirit.
Bern Williams

- You can't be happy or successful until you know what you really want.

- Once you know what you want, you have to know what it is worth to you.

- Each person must define success in their own way and on their own terms.

- Invest in yourself and your own personal growth to achieve your dreams.

- Do something that you love and are passionate about.

- Don't focus so much on getting that signature on the dotted line. Instead, focus on how you can be of service to your clients.

- Action trumps perfection.

CHAPTER 7

YOUR DIRECTION

Set your course by the stars, not by the lights of every passing ship.
American General Omar Bradley

The end of any year is a time for reflection, introspection and planning. We readily contemplate the new year ahead and make projections as to what we want to accomplish. The milestones of business such as increased sales, productivity and profit margin, as well as the personal goals to live healthier and improve our quality of life take center stage. We may reflect on the past year with mixed emotions, we likely accomplished a great deal, but perhaps not everything that we set out to a year prior, but still we have hope for the new year as a time to re-focus and make improvements.

Unfortunately, for many of us, before the month of January has even come to a close, our enthusiasm toward making the changes necessary to facilitate our progress, is long forgotten. Shoved aside by the tyranny of the seemingly urgent issues of the day, they are quickly relegated to 'hopes' rather than goals that we are consciously working toward. By the time February arrives, we have already reverted back to our dominant paradigms, our old pattern of thoughts and old actions (or lack of action) - and of course we get the same old results. It doesn't have to be this way!

Does the above scenario sound familiar to you? If it does, and you are ready to admit it, this is a great first step toward making a positive change. You see, every one of us, without exception, could make improvements in our lives, businesses or careers and relationships.

If you find yourself caught in this seemingly endless cycle of life, you are certainly not alone. While most people understand that in order to achieve, they have to first set a goal, too many people fail to recognize that stating a goal is not the same as setting a goal. While it may seem to be a case of mere semantics, in reality the nuance between the two is significant. In fact there is such a great misunderstanding in the considerable differences, that it can, in most scenarios mean the difference between success and failure. Our focus over the next few pages will be on setting effective goals, while in the following chapter, we will examine actual achievement, but bear in mind that both are vital to progress and of course the end result.

I am often approached and asked, "How do I set goals?" While it seems a simple question, they ask this because it is at times a challenge to get right. Frankly, it is quite surprising how many people don't know why and how to set the right goal. Many of you, and certainly anyone who has taken a business course, has likely heard the S-M-A-R-T goals formula. This formula states that goals should be specific, measurable, attainable, realistic, and timely. While there is certainly some sound advice to be found in this acronym, there are certain components that need to be modified for you to really achieve your objectives, goals and dreams. Let's start with where I agree with the formula. It is true that all goals should be specific, measurable and timely. For example, you cannot merely say, "I'm going to be wealthy" or "I want my business to be successful." You must be specific.

How much money exactly constitutes wealth in your mind and what do you want it for? What does it mean to say your business is successful – does that mean more total sales, larger profit margins or expansion? It's a helpful exercise to first consider what lies beneath your desire. What are you really after? What are the materialistic things that you would buy with the money that you seek? What will a more successful business mean to you? Knowing and understanding your motives will assist and benefit you in becoming emotionally involved with your goal, thus moving you closer to achieving your goal, no matter what that may be.

Making a goal measurable is essential so that you know where you stand at any given moment, and how far you have to go. You also need to know when you have achieved your goal. If you have no idea on the exact endpoint or result, then it is too vague to actually motivate you.

The timeline is also important as it forces you to have a completion date. When you set a specific and measurable goal, then assigning a precise date and time of completion gives it context in your life. The truth is that if there's no timeline put into place, most people will stretch it out forever, putting off the steps necessary to move forward in a concrete way. If we do not set a timeline, most of us usually give ourselves too much time. It's human nature to stretch a task or project to fill all the time allotted rather than finish as quickly as possible. Most of us are deadline driven and we prioritize our activities based on what must be completed first.

Although some of the SMART ideas are helpful, in reality, the idea of an attainable or realistic goal carries some weight, but we have typically been taught not to think too big, or that we shouldn't take risks. We are told not to aim too high just in case we fail, and guess what usually happens... we fail. Just think, how big is the risk that we take when we think small? How many amazing and life changing opportunities are we missing out on, as a result of our paradigm of thinking small? It takes no more energy or effort to think big then it does to think small. While these areas are well intentioned, they do not allow unrestrictive or innovative thought. In order to make quantitative leaps in your life you must be able to envision an extraordinary life for yourself – even if you have no idea how you will achieve it. As you now know from reading this book so far, every goal that you set for yourself is attainable. You can absolutely achieve anything that you can think of. In his book *Think and Grow Rich*, Napoleon Hill states, "What the mind of man can conceive and believe, it can achieve." So again, you can achieve anything that you can think of, without question. There are no exceptions! There are no limits to the capabilities of the human mind and therefore, no limit to the ideas that you can create and no limit in your ability to achieve them. Well, with the exception of the limits that we consciously or unconsciously place upon ourselves.

Let's discuss the 'realistic' aspect of the SMART goals for a moment. We have been told, likely for our entire lives to "be realistic." This can be, and usually is, construed as limiting and can restrict you in your desire to achieve more. Reality is what we make of it, and your reality right now is probably much different than it was ten or even twenty years ago. In fact, if you were to think of yourself back then, would you have imagined the life you have now to be a realistic goal? No matter where you are in your life today, stop worrying about being "realistic," stop impeding yourself when formulating your goals. Stop limiting what you think you can achieve. You must stretch yourself beyond your current situation and skill level – push out of your safe zone into the world of what is possible, rather than probable!

Setting goals high is a priority, as it will force you to quickly attain the skills and resources necessary to fulfill it. In fact, I at times, recommend that you take your goals and double them. For example, if you have a monetary goal to make $100,000 a year, why not make it $200,000? If owning a 2,000 square foot home is one of your goals, why not make it 4,000? If you want to open a new business location next year, why not make it two?

Don't tame your expectations before you even start, or edit your goals based on what you think you can achieve right now. If you approach life with a mentality of what you know you are indubitably able to acquire, you will not approach life with the commitment to act upon what you *want*. That's the difference between an ordinary existence and extraordinary one. It comes down to your goals.

Setting goals creates a road map that every single one of us needs in order to achieve or move our lives to a higher level. Keep in mind the goals that I'm speaking about are not necessarily monetary or materialistic – they are also about our quality of life and how we choose to live. You may even be considering downsizing from your family home and buying a vacation home on a tropical island, or divesting yourself of your current business to start another – whatever the dream, you can only get there by creating a strategy to do so.

This brings us to what distinguishes merely *stating* a goal from actually *setting* a goal. In setting a goal, you need to understand that it's necessary for you to make a decision, not just lip service. This is not a decision to be taken lightly. You must make an *irrevocable* decision! Not a hope, not a dream, but a commitment to make it happen. In other words, you need to make a decision that you cannot reverse.

You know the old saying, "Don't burn your bridges?" Well, I'm now telling you to ignore that advice. In order to make an irrevocable decision, you must burn the bridges behind you and allow yourself no alternative but to move forward. This is absolutely necessary if you are to achieve these new and fulfilling goals. If you do not replace the habits and routines that got you to your current state of being, then you will likely revert back into this pattern when things get difficult, and therefore fail in your quest to achieve your goals. If you fail to make an irrevocable decision, you are not ready to receive whatever it is that you are seeking, that which you most deeply desire.

This is not to suggest you won't encounter obstacles. You likely will, but each obstacle is a necessary part of the process. There may be doubts and challenges that will attempt to undermine your commitment on occasion, but these are also just part of the journey and you have to resolve at the beginning not to allow these things to hinder your progress. Many times when setting goals, we will think of a goal but at the same time we mentally put an asterisk on it that gives us an out. We will do all we can, but not really devote significant time and effort to the project. Or maybe we'll work on it if it's cheap or doesn't cost us much. Or we will focus until it gets really difficult, then we'll allow ourselves to give up. You cannot pick a stopping point, allow yourself to only give a half effort and call it good.

A part of the goal setting process naturally includes some introspection. You have to stop offering platitudes and excuses for why you haven't achieved goals you have set in the past. Be honest and call a spade a spade. Being dishonest with yourself isn't getting you anywhere, and if you haven't made the progress that you desire, you must stop and figure out why, then resolve to fix it.

When we are engaged in goal setting, we also must stop over thinking and dissecting things to death. This syndrome is known as 'analysis paralysis' and it is rampant among those that aspire to be high achievers. If they can't see every step in the process, they wait and gather more information until they discover they have wasted literally years, and still have made little, if any progress. Go as far as you can see right now. The road to your goal may be long and winding and there is no such thing as a perfect situation, life is always changing. You will not always be able to see what lies ahead until you turn the corner directly in front of you. If you can make that irrevocable decision, actually take that first step, then you will be shown the next step in the process and so on. In time, you will find that you have achieved more than you ever dreamed possible at the onset. You may not even realize it until after you have achieved your goals. In fact, that's exactly what happened to me.

I had for many years wanted to purchase a new car, something unique and special. This was a dream of mine for probably twenty years. I assure you, twenty years ago, I was in no position to entertain buying anything of the sort. But I now realize that, like many people do, I was looking at my goal the wrong way. I had no idea the potential I had or how to use this to truly achieve what I wanted in life. By the way, I did finally achieve my goal a few years ago, and purchased the car that I had envisioned.

Most of us see or envision something that we want, and think, "I'd truly like to have or achieve that, but..." or we see something that we want, and think, "Someday, maybe, I'll be able to have that." This goes back to what I mentioned earlier. Most of us never see ourselves already in possession of the objects of our desire. We may see other people with what we want and say, "I wish I could have that. That would be so wonderful. But I can't. I don't know how."

I can tell you from experience that one of the most important things that you can do when setting a goal like this, is to forget about the 'how.' Most of us become so focused on the how, that we close our minds to the opportunities that are all around us, and that are being presented to us as a piece of the puzzle in achieving our "big picture" goal. If we would just focus on what we want, and set the goal, that is, make an irrevocable decision, then we would recognize the possible solutions to the obstacles that we may encounter. It just takes the right frame of mind. It takes directing our thoughts in the right places. When you focus on the how, you naturally become focused on all of the potential things that could go wrong – all the 'what if's.' In doing this, you convince yourself that you are setting out on a losing proposition. This undermines every action you take, because now you believe that the odds of you achieving your goals are quite long indeed. This is what happened with my desire to own a unique car. In the beginning it was more a hope rather than a goal, and therefore I really never did anything, or focus on what I needed to do to make it happen.

A few years ago, I finally brought home the car I had wanted for years. It wasn't until I really understood that it was possible, that I was able to achieve it. I changed my mindset. I focused on my goal. I made an irrevocable decision to achieve it. I shifted my thinking from "someday I wish I could" or "someday maybe I will" to "That's my car!" In a relatively short period of time from when I first changed my mindset, I was able to change my results. I realize now that I could have achieved this and much more considerably sooner, and once I decided, the accomplishment of the goal was much easier than I ever imagined. In fact now I look back and wonder, "What was I thinking?" It wasn't that big of a deal, but in my mind I was convinced it was so far out of the realm of possibility that I didn't think it would ever happen, and it didn't for almost 20 years!

When I am working with students and clients, in a one-on-one scenario, they will often consider a goal but then say, "Shawn, it's impossible. I can't do it."

Perhaps they are talking about starting a new business. Possibly they are thinking about buying a new car or maybe they are talking about buying a new home. Maybe they are even talking about buying a cabin on the lake. Maybe it's true love they seek. It truthfully doesn't matter.

When they say, "It's impossible. I can't do it."

I typically say, "You're right."

They look at me stunned.

If that is their mindset from the beginning, whatever *it* is, then they have already established their outcome. They already know what their result is going to be. They are not going to get what they want. That's really the bottom line. If you haphazardly throw out a goal and the mere mention of it evokes a defeatist attitude, then no matter what you desire, you will surely be defeated. We talked about this a little earlier, you should be focused on the big picture goal, the end result, what you are truly seeking in your life, business and relationships. If you are focused on defeat and failure as the end result, what are your chances of succeeding?

Most of us are unable to see this fundamental truth because, sadly, we weren't raised that way. We were taught, "We should only to believe what we see. If we don't see it, we don't believe it." This is a fallacy. Furthermore, this is backward – if you can only achieve what you can see, how would you ever move forward? Everything around you was at one time only an idea in somebody's mind. Many of those ideas were discarded as "impossible." Take the computer you work on each day. Bill Gates was told it was ridiculous to think everyone would have a use for this machine. What about the cell phone you use? Thirty years ago the idea of selling 'air time' was ridiculous, yet our lives are permeated by these items that were just ideas a short time ago. You have to decide if you will limit your potential and your life, or not. While we may feel like we are limited by events or circumstances, we are really only limited by our own minds and what we think we can achieve.

Now it's your turn. Set a goal by making an irrevocable decision and watch what happens. Here is an example of the principle in action. When I cover this topic in my seminars, I ask the following question: "How many people in this room have gone out and bought a home?" Most of the hands in the room go up. I then ask: "How many of you started the process of buying a home by committing $1,000 or $2,000 in earnest money, while not knowing where the rest of the down payment was going to come from until just prior to closing day?" On average about half of the hands in the room go up. They immediately start to see the point.

When you sign an offer to purchase a home, you are making an irrevocable decision. Sure you may set conditions, like making sure that the inspector goes through the house or being approved at the bank, but essentially you are making an irrevocable decision to move forward with your purchase.

Whether it was a $200,000 home, a $1 million piece of property or something of greater value, you were agreeing to buy it by committing your earnest money. But guess what? When it came time for the rest of the down payment, even if you didn't know where it was going to come from at the time your offer was accepted, I'm willing to wager that you were able to come up with the remainder of the required funds on, or just prior to closing day.

Why? Because you made an irrevocable decision. You committed. You became emotionally involved. You didn't leave yourself a fallback option. You didn't allow yourself the luxury of going back on your commitment, of going back to your comfort zone or security blanket. You didn't leave yourself any option other than to come up with the money. That is how you truly set a goal and force yourself to achieve it.

Now make no mistake, it's not enough just to set a goal and passively wait for all of your dreams to come true. It will take effort and a great deal of ACTION. You will be presented with challenges. It will be a matter of staying focused on your goal after you have made that irrevocable decision, and actively working toward solutions to make it a reality, to achieve it in physical form.

It will be an ongoing campaign. From time to time, all of us struggle to remain focused on our goal. While it is certainly a natural occurrence, the truth is that if we want to achieve what it is we truly desire, we all need to stop worrying about the "what-ifs" and push through to achieving what we want. Again, the Law of Action always applies. You are going to have to undo that seatbelt and get off the sofa. Once you do, once you make that irrevocable decision, you will be amazed at how your "luck" turns around. Execution is key!

My father used to say: "The harder I work, the luckier I get." There is a lot of wisdom behind that idea, because as long as we are stepping out into the unknown and actively seeking the opportunities to bring our dreams to fruition, we will be presented with answers.

In our new "Power of A" - Strategic Accountability coaching program, we actually talk about working smarter, not harder. You see, I'm not in any way suggesting that you have to work harder than you currently are in order to get ahead. But I do like this catch phrase because it implies that there is really no such thing as luck.

Don't permit yourself to feel as though you are a victim! Circumstances are typically only temporary, and we likely had some involvement in our current situation. Empower yourself by refocusing on your goals and the reasons that you chose these goals in the first place. This will allow you to control your own success, or the opposite. Like nearly everything else in life, It's your decision. You are ultimately responsible for the results in your life.

People also come up to me from time to time and they say "Shawn, I set a goal, but I'm not seeing any positive results."

I say, "Then you haven't made an irrevocable decision."

They look and me and say, "Yes, I have."

I say, "No, you haven't. Because if you had made an irrevocable decision in pursuit of your goal, then you would be seeing some positive results in your life." It's the combined power of the Laws of Action and Attraction that bring about the change. Simply, it's being accountable to yourself first, and then to your mentor or coach. Work with your coach collaboratively to outline a systematic approach and plan.

I assure you this will work if its completed correctly, and you follow it through to achievement. If you don't have a coach, do yourself a favor and get one. You are worth the investment, and with the right coach, you will experience the success you desire. Don't hesitate, you don't want to miss any opportunities, just go and do it. You will be happy that you did. You cannot put a price on success!

Making an irrevocable decision means that you cannot have any conflicting thoughts in your mind. You are certain in your ability to achieve your dreams, and you are actively moving forward in pursuit of them. I'm not saying that you have all the answers, but you are at least certain in your ability to achieve whatever it is you want in life.

Ultimately, what we need to understand is that most of us, when sitting down to outline our future, remain locked inside our current paradigms or our current way of thinking. The typical way we set goals comes as a result of a lot of our preconditioning. Now you can change all that. You can start thinking in terms outside of the limiting realm of your past. There is no limit to what you can imagine and therefore no limit to what you can do.

Think of it this way: What would you do if you knew you couldn't fail? Not what would you do if you *thought* it was realistic, but what would you do if you knew that failure was impossible? Take a moment to really think about this.

This is where the mental faculty of imagination comes in. In order to create a goal in keeping with what you truly want, you must learn to rely on this powerful tool. As children we utilized our imagination a great deal, but as we left childhood behind we put a cap on our creative abilities.

This is the time to tap into this faculty that was suppressed as a child. You may remember hearing people say when you were young, "stop daydreaming!" Now is your time to unleash those natural abilities that were nearly extinguished.

The dreamers are the builders. We need to unleash this amazing and phenomenal tool as we likely haven't used it to its full potential in quite some time, if ever. Exercise it, let it wander. I assure you that the outcome will shock and amaze you. Granted it may take you a little time to get the hang of it again, as your imagination probably hasn't been out of the box in a few years. I urge you to spend a little time each day allowing yourself to envision your objectives. Contrary to what some of us have been told, and perhaps believe, dreams do come true. Let your imagination soar!

So often we make this process much harder than it needs to be and we erect our own barriers. It is important to think creatively and set goals that are lofty and that inspire you. Whether you are an individual trying to take your personal life to a new level, or the president and CEO of a company striving toward getting your team to soar to new heights, it's imperative that you understand the effect that the correct goal and that an irrevocable decision can have on an individual's motivation and purpose. There are a number of motivators, but one of the best and most effective are our successes. Achievement is a motivator. This not only keeps us going along the path to our dreams, it also motivates those around us to help us along the way.

One of the biggest impediments to success, is the notion that you will put off setting your destination until the time is right, or until the end of the year, or until you really have the time. This never works! Don't wait for circumstances to change. Start now by setting goals that you want to become emotionally involved with. Don't procrastinate. Procrastination is the polar opposite of accountability and action. If you have a goal, regardless of what it is, start now! Don't wait. I'm not saying that you will be able to completely reach your destination in one day, but you can start the process and be much further along the path.

Whether it's within your current organization, whether it's with respect to your family, or within your immediate scope of influence, you must start from where you are right now, and not wait until everything aligns or is perfect. This is something that's incredibly important to understand: You can spearhead change from right where you are. You don't need to have a specific title or have reached a certain milestone in your life. You don't have to wait until someone gives you permission to change your life, only you can make that decision, and when you continue on your current path, then only you have made the decision not to change. You are not trapped in the life you currently lead – no one is, and if you feel that way, realize that is just perception not reality.

Okay lets go back to the Law of Action for a few moments, you have to get up off your backside and work your plan for you to show any noteworthy gains. I'll admit that at times this can seem arduous, especially when you go through a very vexing period in your life. For example; if you get laid off. Even the C-suite team can go through this particular trial, and odds are you may experience something like this more than once in a lifetime. At times like this, your life can seem bleak and without a future, and you can very easily slip into panic mode.

While you may feel dejected or betrayed by circumstances, there is always another path that opens to offer you a better and or more viable option. Everything does happen for a reason, and everything has a purpose. Perhaps you have thought about or even investigated starting your own company, and now the layoff has given you the motivation to finally do it. Always seek solutions and they will appear, but if you give in to fear and doubt, you will just spiral downward. Always look for the opportunity in every situation, notwithstanding how impossible it may initially appear.

As we talked about in chapter one, Napoleon Hill said that you must have a near obsession and a burning desire in order to achieve what you truly want. This will eliminate much confusion, anxiety, fear and doubt as you advance headlong toward your goal. But you must think way beyond what you know or think is probable in determining what you want, and then make the irrevocable decision to pursue it. By doing so, you will already have taken a quantum leap toward turning your dream into a reality. Remember, possible and not probable!

You may be thinking, "It can't be this easy." Well again, the road will not necessarily appear to be easy, but you most certainly can do it. Not because I said it is so, but because it has been proven many times over, and more importantly, it's the truth. When you focus on where you are going instead of getting bogged down in what you may perceive as problems or challenges, solutions become available to you that will allow you to move forward in a positive way, even if it initially seems impossible. Once you have created the road map by setting the right goal and making that irrevocable decision, you are moving forward in the direction of your goal. You have commenced and are underway. It is now imperative that you stay on course. Don't be swayed by every little test or adversity that may come your way. Always remain laser focused on your goal.

CHAPTER 7
YOUR DIRECTION

Either you run the day or the day runs you.
Jim Rohn

• Stating a goal is not the same as setting a goal, and setting a goal is not the same as achieving a goal.

• Goals should be specific, measurable and timely.

• There are no limits to what you can achieve.

• You must push past what you feel is probable and focus on what is possible.

• Setting goals high will force you to quickly attain the skills and resources necessary to fulfill them.

• You will not always see what lies ahead until you turn the corner directly in front of you.

• Exercise your Faculty of WILL: Focus on your goals and objectives to the exclusion of all outside distractions.

CHAPTER 8

ACHIEVEMENT

The more intensely we feel about an idea or a goal, the more assuredly the idea, buried deep in our subconscious, will direct us along the path to its fulfillment.
Earl Nightingale

Now that we have firmly established and understand the goal setting process, it's time to shift our focus on the all important aspect of actually achieving those goals. There is certainly some overlap within the two areas, in order to achieve your goals efficiently and in a timely manner, they among other things, must bet set accurately and precisely.

The most vital aspect is to ensure that you make an irrevocable decision and stick to it, don't let the 'how' part of the equation distract you. The tools and resources will be available for you to move toward your goal, but you have to take the first steps on faith. This is faith based on the belief that you will succeed, and the confidence that you have in yourself.

Accomplishing the goals that you have set, boils down to one thing – accountability. Not making excuses or letting life get in the way. You must force yourself to focus, this is a true force of will. We, by nature, get comfortable and at times tend to slack off in many areas, so you have to be hyper vigilant to ensure your sustained progress, and of course, eventual success. You must hold yourself accountable if you want to achieve your goals. Should you need some assistance and support, which we all do from time to time, you should work with a coach that will help you become and remain accountable.

I have clients that I am currently assisting in the accountability aspect as it relates to the universal laws that assist us in achievement. These are great people that I just recently started working with. We had a number of conversations prior to deciding to work together. Each time that we talked, they described in great detail some kind of catastrophe in either their lives or their business. They were keenly aware that there needed to be change, they just couldn't figure out what needed to change, or how to start. Something always seemed to have gone wrong. And whom did they say was responsible for the described and perceived challenges? Everybody and anybody but themselves. It was always someone else's "fault." The staff either didn't do something or didn't do it correctly, a family member caused the issue that created this problem or that challenge. In reality, it wasn't their environment or the people that formed a part of the problem, it was the fact that they never took responsibility for their actions or for what went on in their lives.

There are two types of people and you have to decide which one you are going to be. Are you going to be a victim or are you going to be responsible for your own life? It can be a little intimidating to accept full responsibility. You see, as long as you can blame someone or something else, you don't have to fix it and you can fool yourself into thinking that "it's not me." When you choose to accept full responsibility for everything in your life, that means you are responsible to fix it or respond in the best manner possible, and we often don't relish that. It is easier to point the finger outward than at ourselves. In order to really make a change in your life and your thoughts, you must focus on what you can do to improve, and then do it.

A lot of people fail to make the connection between the thoughts that they project onto others through blame and the negativity that is brought into their own lives as a result. In effect, they are wallowing in self-pity and self-disgust and trying to shift focus away from all they are choosing not to do. If you constantly choose to blame, you prevent yourself from seeing the opportunities, as you will be cultivating a negative outlook and a closed mindset.

If you are focused on all the negative aspects that you have brought into your life to date, what do you think will be in store for your future? How can you possibly expect, and more importantly attain, different and improved results? Here's another important question to ponder: What are you regularly attracting into your life on a daily basis? That will give you the answer as to where your thoughts are and what you need to change, if you are still unsure then look at your current results as they are a direct product of your thought process. If you are today focused on the negative, you will without question bring more of the same into your life in the future.

It's a vicious cycle, and one in which many of us continue to travel, although it is the same drivel repeating itself again and again. Until we break that cycle, we are doomed to repeat the failures of our past and remain stuck with that gnawing feeling of dissatisfaction in our lives both today and into the future. As a society, and individually, we are so focused on what it is we *don't* want, that we are prevented from discovering what it is we *do* want most of the time. We clog our days and occupy our minds with so many toxic thoughts and potentially damaging diversions, that it is virtually impossible to focus on what we truly seek and the direction in which we want to travel. Think of your mind for a moment as a container of ideas, and if its full, then something has to come out before more can be put in. You must eliminate your negative debilitating thoughts and consciously choose to replace them with positive ideas and beneficial ideals.

Even if we know we shouldn't be promulgating unsubstantiated negative or harmful information about others, it doesn't seem to be enough to stop us from doing it. Some of us still continue to gossip and spread more poisonous ideas and inaccuracies. We may even preface our destructive comments with a disclaimer. We may say, "I know I shouldn't be talking about this, but guess what they did? They lied to their vendors and refused to pay until they were threatened with legal action." So what. No one really wants to hear it, and your mind doesn't have room to keep spewing it. The words and actions of others should have nothing to do with your success in life. You are responsible for the results you get, and it makes no difference what anyone else does or says – if they are with you or against you. You make the decisions. You are in control, you are in the driver's seat. So, decide what you need to do and go do it. Don't allow negative thoughts or destructive individuals to stand in the way of you achieving your goals.

Getting back to the previous example of my new clients in relation to accountability and the Laws of Action and Attraction, the minute they made the irrevocable decision to change their mindset, they began to see improvements. When they set a goal and focused on what they wanted to happen instead of what they did not want to happen, they saw those thoughts and ideals manifest. The moment they changed their mindset, they changed their results. They recently received a phone call and were awarded a contract on which they had bid months earlier. This deal is going to pay them somewhere close to $300,000. See what can happen when your focus changes? The clients called me that afternoon very excited to see tangible results. Will it work in your life, in your business or career and relationships? Absolutely!

As I already mentioned, there is a direct correlation between setting the correct goals, and your ability to achieve them. You must become emotionally involved with each goal, almost to the level of obsession. By doing this, you will have actually already achieved that goal on the first level, because you will have achieved it in your mind. Remember, your subconscious mind makes no distinction between the inside world and the outside world. It's incapable of doing so. The reality of your unconscious mind is absolute, so when you visualize something in the present, you have already achieved your goal on the first level. Your subconscious mind doesn't know the difference between reality and imagination. Professional athletes have known this fact for decades and regularly focus their minds on how they will perform. Golfers see themselves birdie difficult holes. Basketball players see themselves sinking every free-throw. Hockey players see themselves make the perfect shot and scoring. Just as it works for them, exercising your accomplishments in your mind will work for you.

To make the best use of the power this type of idea can have, it is also important to frame your goal statement in the present tense. You must see yourself already in possession of your goal – as if it has already happened. Now hang on to that emotion. Relive it over and over; what it feels like to achieve your goal. Acting as if you have already achieved your goals will allow your subconscious mind to manifest things that are consistent with that reality, thereby actually bringing that goal into physical form.

Let's say that your goal is to be the top salesperson in your company. You then need to answer these questions about that title holder: How would that person act? How would that person talk? How would that person dress? What would that person do differently? If you can adopt the behavior of the top salesperson in your company, then you will begin to realize the results of the top salesperson in your company. If this is one of your goals, you need to first make the irrevocable decision that you are the top salesperson in your company, and start to act like it.

Bob Proctor has another way of putting it. He regularly refers to the act of making an irrevocable decision as "planting a seed." This directly ties into the Law of Gestation, which decrees that every seed has an incubation or gestation period. It takes time for a seed to germinate and sprout —but, nevertheless, it will grow once planted.

We, from time to time, become disillusioned. We set a goal and we do what we determine is necessary in order to achieve our goal for a short amount of time, and when it doesn't manifest in the timeframe that we have determined appropriate, we give up. We abandon our goals. You see this with many New Year's resolutions, or new company objectives set at the beginning of the fiscal year – in a great many cases, a month later they are a distant memory. It's true, you need to set a time period in which you will achieve your goals. If you do not reach it in that specified amount of time, don't throw in the towel. This is when you want to reevaluate all aspects of the situation, your goal and how you got to where you are, then rededicate yourself and expand your efforts. There are no excuses, now go and get it done!

If you plant a seed in fertile soil, (i.e., your subconscious mind), cultivate it (get emotionally involved) thus allowing it to grow, you will witness something amazing, that goal ultimately will materialize. It will move into physical form. It's the law. It's undeniable. It will happen. You just have to act pursuant to your plan over a sufficient period of time. You can't expect to set grandiose plans and achieve them the next day – grand plans take time.

You will find, and it is likely that you will deviate from time to time, don't beat yourself up over it. As human beings, it is natural for brief periods, to lose focus and at times, sight of your goals. The psycho-cybernetic mechanism, or your auto pilot, referred to by Dr. Maxwell Maltz, will bring you back on target. You will refocus on your objective, your big picture or A1 goal, on the thing or things that you are seeking and that are important to you.

If you are clear on your objective, if you are focused on your objective, and if you are truly dedicated to achieving your objective, you will succeed. It is completely irrelevant whether those goals are of a personal nature, of a business or career emphasis, or perhaps on relationships, you can make it happen. One more component, and we've talked about it before, it's the action or execution piece of the puzzle. You have to be accountable to yourself and your coach. You need to be motivated and you have to act! One of the best ways to remain focused on your goals, is to carry a goal card and read it several times each day. This is a highly effective way to ensure that your goal is at the forefront of your thoughts throughout the day. You can carry the goal card in your purse, in your pocket, or wherever works bests for you. Every time you touch the card, it will spark an image of your goal on the screen of your mind. In fact, even if you never *see* the card, it's going to continuously spark an image of your goal on the screen of your mind throughout your day. Again, the more specific the goal on your card, the better.

Bob Proctor likes to say that "way down deep inside of you is a dream. Every now and then, that dream floats to the surface of your conscious mind and when it does, you quickly push it out and say, 'I can't do it'. The truth is, you can do it, you just haven't made the decision to do it yet." Having a goal card, to keep you focused is one sure way to help you achieve your desired results.

Along the way to your larger destination, you will reach and accomplish many of the smaller goals that you have set for yourself. If you want to follow through and achieve your goals, then from the moment you set them, you need to be doing your part in keeping the soil of your mind weed free. You must immediately act as if you have already achieved your goal. You do that by focusing on your goal, by believing in it and staying emotionally involved by seeing yourself already in possession of it.

Again, the subconscious mind doesn't know the difference. The subconscious mind doesn't know that you don't already have the car that you desire. Impressing the idea on your subconscious mind is actually the first step in converting that idea into physical form. You must see yourself in physical possession of the object of your desire. It does work. It's a powerful force. As such, you must recognize that just as the rule applies in the positive sense, it also applies in the negative sense. Remember, happiness and peace of mind are not goals, they are the direct result of achieving big huge and gratifying goals.

Components of achievement and the true meaning of success.

Happiness and peace of mind are not goals, they are the result of achieving BHAG's (Big Hairy Audacious Goals).

I recently had a woman from Australia contact me. We were talking about her business and she said "there's just no business. It's dead. There's nobody out there that needs my services right now."

Now let me ask you something: how many new clients do you think this person will attract and make a sale to with that kind of attitude? It goes back to what I said earlier, if somebody tells me that they can't do something, I tell them they're right. They're right because the subconscious mind will convert their internal reality into an external reality. The same applies in every aspect of your life, both personal and professional. If you say there's no business out there, then you're right. If you say you can't do something about your situation, you're right.

Now I'm not arguing against the notion that a great many are experiencing difficult times, or that you may be faced with significant challenges. Far from it. We all go through legitimate rough patches in our lives. This is definitely a part of the cycle that is life. The point here is that some people will argue that if the Law of Attraction is in play, then they can just sit back and wait for the business to come to them. Well, that is definitely not the case. That's not how it works. There's more to it than that. While it's true that you must invoke the Law of Attraction, establishing a positive vibration, it's also true that you then have to invoke the Law of Action to get things moving.

The problem is many of us never get past the first part. We get complacent, perhaps even lazy. We've watched a movie or read a book, and think that will be enough for us to achieve our goals. We think we can then relax and let the Law of Attraction take over, thinking positive thoughts and waiting for all the good things to flood into our lives. While movies and books such as the worldwide phenomenon *The Secret* are a fantastic source of inspiration and some knowledge, there is more to the story. I give Rhonda Byrne a lot of credit for putting together this book and movie, because it opened people's eyes. There are a staggering number of people that have seen the movie or read the book who have been positively affected by it. She has obviously struck a chord. The book and the movie give you a much needed foundation, but leave the audience hanging a little bit, as it doesn't go very far into the action part of the equation. We need to build on that foundation. There is more to achieving what it is you want in life than just setting a goal. That's a big part of it, don't get me wrong, but in order to build a house that's going to stand for a few years, you need both the foundation and the supporting structure.

You are capable of achieving anything that you set your mind to. But there's a key to it. On the bestselling recording *The Strangest Secret*, Earl Nightingale asserts that you cannot have a goal and conflicting thoughts at the same time, and still expect to achieve that goal. He instructed us to stay focused on our goals, on what we truly desire, in order to fulfill those aspirations. Wallace D. Wattle stated that we have to do certain things in a "certain way" in order to reach our destination. If you want to achieve your dreams, you must remain unequivocal in your beliefs. After all, how can you possibly expect to achieve anything in life if you are always contradicting yourself? The problem is most of us do have conflicting thoughts, and in some instances, doubts.

You can't just tepidly say, "I guess I can achieve a goal of earning a million dollars," while in the back of your mind, you are thinking "No I can't. It's impossible. I don't have the ability to do this. My dad didn't. My grandfather didn't. So I can't."

Again, as you already know, this is generational thinking. We have grown up with these paradigms. For the most part, the information upon which we base our thoughts and decisions has been passed down to us. This way of thinking is regressive and becomes a major hurdle for many people in ever achieving their dreams. Remember: if you are not moving forward you are moving backward, there is no such thing as stagnation. So you must eliminate conflicting thoughts and work diligently toward mastering your understanding and awareness of the laws of the universe under which we operate and benefit. As much of an advantage as you can derive from hard work, if you are to make great strides toward achieving your dreams, you must also utilize your mind fully.

Everybody can work a little bit harder and make a little bit more. If you make $100,000 a year today and you want to make $120,000 next year, you can work a little bit harder, and you can bump up your earnings incrementally. We are not talking about doing it in increments. We are talking about making a quantum leap - quickly going from where you are today to where you want to be in the very near future. This is not a get rich quick scheme. As Wallace D. Wattles said, you just have to do specific things in a "certain way" in order to make it happen. I was able to go from making $15,000 a year to in excess of $200,000 a year in a very short period of time. I went from living in a rented run-down apartment, to living in a house that I built. I kept going from there. It works. There is absolutely no reason why you, or anybody else, cannot make a jump in a similar fashion.

It's all a matter of deciding what you want, and making an irrevocable decision to do what you need to do in order realize your dreams. It's extremely important to never violate the rights of other people and to always stay within the boundaries of the law. I'm talking about doing whatever is necessary within your power and control.

If you actually made the irrevocable decision to proceed with whatever your objectives or goals are, there will come a time where you will have achieved them. Getting there though, is something that we need to stay focused on. I'm not talking about having the roadmap laid out in front of you like a global positioning system. What I'm talking about is having the confidence, conviction and perseverance to keep going, realizing that the next step will be shown to you. In other words, as previously mentioned, forget about the "how." You must understand that what you need will come. This involves risk – the risk of failure and of stepping into the unknown with no safety net. If you seek safety, then you will never live the life you really desire. You have to choose – risk for reward or safety for sameness.

No one has ever achieved anything worthwhile in life that was easy. In that sense, achieving your goal may be, in fact, only a very small part of the overall satisfaction that you receive. The reward of getting to your destination will be much greater as a result of the journey itself.

Along the way, you must keep in mind that you get back what you put in. That's an important part of achieving your goal. So ask yourself: What am I putting out there? I had a client recently say to me, "When I work with a client that pays hourly, I go sixty minutes and that's it. No exceptions. When that sixty minutes has passed—even if we're in the middle of a conversation—we're through."

Now, in my opinion, I feel that is a poor way to conduct business. Sure, we all need to make a living and we all value our time. But if you really want that little extra in life, putting that little extra out there is the way to get it back. Above all, the satisfaction you receive is a feeling unlike anything else.

I'm not saying that you should do it selfishly, always expecting something in return. But I would suggest putting in that little extra effort because it's the right thing to do, in more ways than one. Hold yourself to a higher standard. If it takes you an extra ten or fifteen minutes to complete a task, so what. I assure you that in the end, it will come back to you—in more ways than you may be able to fathom.

Achieving your goals really boils down to one thing: We have to understand that we must be willing to sacrifice in order to get whatever it is we want to get, go wherever it is we want to go, or to be whatever it is we want to be. We have to decide what we are willing to sacrifice in order to achieve our goals because nothing comes without a price. We have all heard the cliché, "there is no free lunch." Achieving your goal will always come at a cost, whether you chose to believe it or not. Those people that rely on the lottery for their retirement plan, will probably never be successful because they are not prepared to make any sacrifices. You must take responsibility for creating your own future and put forth the effort.

I heard a story recently that a gentleman won a multi-million dollar lottery in the springtime a couple of years ago. Before snow started flying in the fall of that same year, he was flat broke. Why? Because he had never been taught about and didn't understand money. He didn't understand the value of a dollar. If you look at people who understand money and understand that it takes a little bit of effort to make money, you will see their remarkable ability to repeatedly earn large sums.

Donald Trump had some financial troubles some years back. He was near bankruptcy. Here is somebody who understands money. In a very short period of time, he had augmented his fortunes to the point where "lack" was a thing of the past. I sometimes refer to this when I'm talking to people, especially in coaching sessions. Many people say, "Yeah, but Trump was born with a silver spoon in his mouth." Well, granted there may have been some of that, but you cannot deny Trump's business savvy and ambition. If you can take multiple companies that are billions of dollars in debt, and you can turn them around and make them profitable again, that says a whole lot about your business acumen and ability to generate money. Sure he has "a" name. But there are lots of people that have names. Many of them went under, never to be heard from again.

There's no difference between you, me, or Donald Trump. Trump has just as many hours in the day as you do. He gets the exact same amount of time as you do. You cannot manage your time, as time is a universal constant, but you can manage your activities. Are you managing your activities? Or are you trying to manage your time? Are you focused on what you truly want? Or are you focused on what other people are saying? Are you focused on what your goals are? Or are you allowing outside sources such as the media tell you what you should be pursuing?

Concentrate on what it is that you truly want in life regardless of what anyone else has to say about it. There are always going to be detractors that try to impede your progress. They may say, "You're crazy. You should want this, not that. How can someone like you have a goal like that?" As you begin to achieve your goals and you reach that level of success you aspire to, there will be people that fade out of your life. I'm not saying that you are not ever going to have contact with them again, but they will retreat from your life to some degree. This happens because success intimidates some individuals and they may feel your success is a reflection on their lack of success. You may even find this among family members because siblings and others may see you as a mirror reflecting their own life, and if you are suddenly much more successful they feel smaller somehow.

Right after I bought my new car, I happened to run into two acquaintances, upon seeing what I was driving they asked, "why'd you buy that piece of junk?" Not because there was anything wrong with the car, but because of what the car represented, which was my moving ahead. It often represents what many people know is true. That they too could have whatever they want, if they would just make an irrevocable decision to go after it. Rather than go after it they find it easier to criticize and tear down your progress. Once you've realized that anything is possible, you know what it is you truly want, and you've made the irrevocable decision to pursue it, you will likely find yourself on a unique path.

Even if you don't see any evidence that someone has been there before you, that's alright. It means that you haven't conformed to the mindset of the masses, and it's also an indication that you are heading in the right direction. In fact, looking around and noticing that you are in the clear should be perceived as a sign that you are headed right toward opportunities and your goal.

CHAPTER 8
ACHIEVEMENT

Setting goals is the first step in turning the invisible into the visible.
Tony Robbins

• You must make an irrevocable decision to reach your goals.

• Do not let the 'how' distract you.

• Accept full responsibility for the actions you take and the decisions you make.

• If you focus on the negative today, you will just bring more of the same into your future.

• You must become emotionally involved with each goal, almost to the point of obsession.

• You can't expect to set grandiose plans and achieve them overnight – grand plans take time.

CHAPTER 9

YOUR ROAD, WITHOUT FOOTPRINTS

Success is not final, failure is not fatal: it is the courage to continue that counts.
Winston Churchill

We all come up with ideas and ambitions. Some of them are grand, while others are modest by comparison. Ideas range from what we're going to have for breakfast in the morning to what we're going to do with the rest of our lives.

When it comes to living a fulfilling life, there remains one obvious difference: Some people act on their ideas, while others bat them around endlessly, perhaps weighing them against a battery of public opinion. Far too many people wait to get confirmation, as to the relevance of their ideas before they would ever dare act upon them. This approach will only be to your detriment. If you genuinely desire to live an extraordinary life, you have to be willing to venture down the road less traveled, regardless of what other people think about your plans.

When I'm in the process of developing a plan or blueprint to pursue, whether in business or my personal life, just like everybody who comes up with a new idea I'm always met with a flood of opinion. Frequently, that deluge will include the usual chorus of detractors. When I hear the familiar sound of people telling me that they believe that my plan is ludicrous, I generally know that I have managed to develop a great idea or concept. When I hear people saying, "Oh no, no…you're crazy…you're way off base," then I know I'm likely onto something. This is because we are so used to being sheep that we have forgotten how to value anything out of the norm. When the whole entire crowd is headed in one direction, I go the opposite way, as that is the path of innovation and dreams. Conformity to the accepted norms is an idea killer.

Again, the biggest killer of creativity is conformity. Unfortunately, a great many of us fall victim to it. We have a predisposition to follow the crowd. We pretty much do what everyone else does, and this has been thrust upon us from our early days of elementary school. Society has instructed us to go about our daily lives in a uniform manner – walk in a straight line, color inside the lines, ask permission before you do anything. I'm not for a moment suggesting that all structure is wrong or that it should be done away with, or that insubordination or disrespect is in any way acceptable. I am, however, stating that this paradigm of conformity creates the conditioning and pre-programming that we carry though most of our lives.

So how do you approach your life? When you have an idea that you know is a winner, do you act on it? Or do you listen to the detractors that are out there saying, "That will never work. You've gone right off the deep end." Are you blindly following the crowd without any creative or conscious thought at all? That's important and something that you ought to consider. For the most part we tend to listen to other people around us and most of these people aren't doing any better than we are – nor do they have any experience taking their own lives to the next level. Listening to them puts us right back on the path to mediocrity, but each of us is capable of more. Every one of us has immense reservoirs of untapped potential deep within us just waiting to be excavated and utilized.

As mentioned earlier, when I told somebody I was going to write a book, I was stunned by the wave of resistance that I encountered: "You're crazy. You can't write a book. What do you know?" This instant pessimism not only came unsolicited from strangers, it also came from some of those people whom I considered close, and who I thought would have been supportive.

We may feel at first that this negative reaction is a result of those we care about trying to protect us. Well, not really. I'm not saying that they don't have a genuine concern for your wellbeing. I'm sure they do. But there are many other reasons why they may be resistant to supporting you in the pursuit of your ideals. Maybe they don't have the ambition that you do. Maybe they don't want you to rise above them. Or maybe they just don't like the idea of you going off and doing something bold. There are a whole host of reasons. Most of the reasons stem from the fact that many people are too fearful to venture outside of their comfort zone, to do something different and perhaps what may seem more difficult, to take a radically different approach and do something way beyond the realm of their paradigm of "normal." In order for you to get extraordinary results, you must do something extraordinary!

Don't let the detractors prevent you from going down the road less traveled. Go after your goals. Go after your dreams.

Don't forget: the dreamers are the builders, the creators and the innovators. Unfortunately, most of us stifle our creative ability and our imagination because we've been directed to conform. This type of indoctrination and programming has been going on around us and to us for many years, likely without us even realizing it. Now it's time to unleash your inherent genius. It's time to use your imagination, that phenomenal gift and mental faculty that you've been given.

Please take a moment to ponder these questions: Are you a follower or are you a leader? Are you the one at the front of the crowd or are you frantically trying to keep up with the pack? Which direction are you headed in? Are you charting your own course? Or are you just taking the widely accepted, pre-navigated option?

Unfortunately, many of us typically settle for the easy route. Why? It's human nature. We typically don't like resistance or possible conflict. We usually seek whatever road will grant us the easiest passage. We follow the path of least resistance. While those roads may at first seem relatively challenge free, I assure you that you will not find success at the end of any of them. They will only lead to a lasting condition of sameness, coupled with many other challenges that accompany an uninspired and lackluster state of being.

There are an infinite number of roads to success, and you can travel any one of them. In fact, many people have actually already been on several of them, only to jump off too soon, never to reach their desired destination. This happens because while there are innumerable roads to success, each can have its own pot holes and speed bumps. These challenges may present major problems and distractions for people. The moment they begin to encounter any bumps along the way, they hop off the road assuming that they shouldn't have been on it in the first place. As I have witnessed over and over again, a great many people jump off because they think that it won't work for them or perhaps they may even believe, wrongly of course, that they don't deserve to live an extraordinary and abundant life.

Stay on that road, ride out the storm, learn from the experiences and use them as you move in the direction of your objectives. For those that opt to jump off, you may come to regret your decision, as you may never reach your destination and had you followed through, notwithstanding a few hardships, you would have eventually reached success faster and been much wiser for the journey. That is something that most of us fail to understand. The road to success was not meant to be easy. Just as you were not meant to live in poverty, you were not meant to go through life without some learning experiences. Once you understand that, you will start to see opportunities all around you, on the road less traveled. By the way, at the time you may think that you can't handle the little tests that will come your way, you will deal with them and be wiser as a result. Be assured, that you will only encounter roadblocks that you can step over, or go around by finding or creating a new path.

It's all about perception. It's not a matter of whether or not you will encounter some rough road and be presented with some interesting challenges – that is a given. It's a matter of how you perceive those challenges that you face, and that perception can be altered for the better or for the worse – it's your choice. Additionally, it's also how you choose to accept and deal with the tests as they come your way, you will pass the tests if that is what you want, and if you are focused on your goal.

At times, it's easy to look at a particular challenge as a mountain rather than merely a speed bump – before you climb over it. You perception is that its HUGE and insurmountable, you wonder how anyone has ever scaled it before. This is the time you must focus and continue to seek solutions. When you are laser focused on the end results, problems will become the solutions that you seek. Soon you are on the other side and now in retrospect, you view that same challenge as a mere speed bump and can hardly believe you ever considered it difficult. You will likely even laugh at how big you made it out to be. This is what I mean about altering your perspective. The challenge itself did not change, but your view of it did, as will your view of all the challenges you face. There is no way to have a contingency plan for every obstacle that may arise, nor should you give any thought to perceived obstacles that have not yet materialized. You should however have the tools to stay focused, and be able work through each little test as it comes.

We've talked about staying focused on our A1 or "big picture" goal, and remaining focused on our objectives to the exclusion of all outside distractions. We've talked about "will," which is one of our intellectual faculties. Again, we are not talking about our ability to force our will on other people. We are talking about our ability to hold an image, the image of our goal, to the exclusion of all outside distractions, regardless of what anyone else has to say about what it is we are doing or the direction in which we are headed. These concepts, like all of the principles in this book, tie together to keep you strong as you head down the road less traveled. That is where you will find the greatest rewards.

We have the ability to accept or reject any thought or idea that comes into our conscious mind. The moment we consciously accept it, it starts to become impressed upon our subconscious mind and therefore, starts to manifest in our lives. So, what is it that you are focused on? What will you manifest in your life? Remember, from time to time you will deviate, but as long as you are focused on your goal and you have replaced an existing habit or paradigm with a new positive and empowering one, you will be brought right back on target.

So, is it going to be a challenge? Are there going to be some stumbling blocks? Absolutely. Are there going to be things that come along that make you ask, "How am I ever going to deal with this?" Of course.

Be mindful of the fact that if you choose to view those challenges as stepping stones rather than stumbling blocks, your journey will be much smoother and achievement much faster. The important thing to remember is that the people who are successful in life, all areas of life, are those that got up one last time after getting kicked down. Get up and keep moving. They are the ones that created their own trail. So often we forget about that. People who are successful are not the "lucky ones" who were able to go through life free from challenges. They are the ones that were willing to take the road less traveled, and do what it took to achieve their dreams. Persistence will pay huge dividends in the end.

Yes, we deserve success. Yes, we deserve prosperity, and yes, we deserve abundance. We deserve great wealth and great health. Again, it is imperative that you understand, getting there is going to take effort, tenacity and determination on your part. The road to success can appear to be a challenging one, and it will continue to be seen in this light. The questions remain: How will you deal with those? How will you perceive those challenges when they are presented to you?

Keep in mind, challenges in and of themselves, do not amount to defeat. This is an inaccuracy that many have bought into. They feel that when they encounter resistance, it's a sign telling them to stop their pursuit. Nothing could be further from the truth.

If you look at challenges as a sign of impending defeat, you will never achieve anything in your life. Nothing worthwhile is free from challenge. In fact, what most people consider "failure" is really just a way of increasing your knowledge. Robert F. Kennedy once said, "Only those who dare to fail greatly can ever achieve greatly." All "failures" are learning experiences. If we never failed in life, we would never achieve anything in life.

I've "lost" and "failed" many times. I've lost hundreds of thousands of dollars over the course of my life. But guess what? I learned a whole lot during the process, and I was able to utilize those lessons to achieve my goals and recover, then prosper.

That is part of what we have to understand. Just because you've failed, doesn't mean you were defeated. You may have lost the battle, but if you continue forward, you can still win the war. That's how you have to look at things. Unfortunately, a lot of us don't. A lot of us go through life afraid of ever encountering any resistance. As soon as we come up against a little bit of a challenge we say, "Forget it." And we go right back to our comfort zone, which in reality is not comforting at all. It's just a state of discontent that we've become accustomed to. And most of us stay there for the rest of our lives. We occasionally look out and take stock of the successful people around us and say, "Wow, they're lucky. He's driving this type of car, she's living in that upscale area, they're yachting in Europe, or that couple has a great marriage."

That could be you. Stop wishing and start creating your path to the life you want, and if any of those things are on your goal list, go after them. You already know that the road less traveled is going to be a challenge. When you overcome those challenges, you will be able to negotiate that path and achieve your goals. As we stated earlier, this means that you must be willing to sacrifice. If you're willing to sacrifice and willing to give that little bit extra, then you will be rewarded handsomely with prosperity and abundance.

As long as you view roadblocks or obstacles as inevitable learning experiences that are easily overcome, then you will have found one of the keys to successfully navigating the road less traveled. There is never going to be a time when you can say, "it's going to be perfect from here." Let me be very clear, your ability to achieve has nothing to do with your educational background, it has nothing to do with where you came from or what your background or cultural identity may be. The majority of it has to do with whether or not you have implemented certain universal laws, which we have already discussed throughout this book.

This is extremely important: So many people prepare for success for an entire lifetime. They are so preoccupied in the preparations, that life and opportunities pass them by. The timing, the situation, the money, the location – it may never be "just right" and it doesn't matter. It's been said that ACTION trumps PERFECTION. Stop preparing for success and take action today, you can achieve success!

There is never going to be a time where you get up from being knocked down and you know that it's the last time that will happen, that this time, you are going to stay on your feet. Success will certainly take some time and it often comes in spurts, usually not long smooth levels. One of the keys to achieving your idea of success is to meet every challenge and every day with the attitude and outlook that you are good enough and you will overcome. This gives you the strength and fortitude to meet any challenge, rather than sliding back into old habits that did not produce the results you really wanted.

One way of directly helping yourself on the road to prosperity, is to remember to focus your efforts on helping others to achieve their dreams. Life is about service, and through service we lift one another higher and higher. It does not matter what business or personal endeavor you are engaged in; if you're willing to give that little bit extra in helping others, it's going to pay tremendous dividends in the end. On *The Strangest Secret*, a recording from 1956, Earl Nightingale went so far as to say that you can always tell the level of service people are providing, by simply driving down their street as they will have achieved prosperity and abundance. Have you ever thought of this test?

Nightingale's point was simply this, those that give more, get more, and where they live is indicative of how much they give. Nightingale's point is well taken. Those that deliver great service, and that are truly focused on the needs of others, will themselves be rewarded with great prosperity and abundance, because that is the way the universe works. Pay it forward, you will get out what you put in.

So as you venture down the road less traveled, maintain your focus and your passion as you encounter every little barrier. You will invariably encounter doubts, but you will know you are on the right path to your goal as your thoughts will always return to that which is most important in your life. Trust your intuition. If you find that you are unable to remain focused on the goal of your choosing, and you are drifting off into other areas, then you know that you are not on the right path. Your "cybernetic mechanism," as Dr. Maxwell Maltz called it, will bring you back to what it is you truly want and desire in life. It will, of course, take some work for you to condition yourself to pursue the right course.

Studies have shown that on average, it takes about twenty-one days for a human being to create a habit. In reality, you will need to replace an existing habit or paradigm with a new one. In this case, the new habit that is being formed (replaced) is the ability to stay constantly focused on your goal. In order to shift your thoughts and ideas, you must consciously do so consistently for a month and this is true of any idea you incorporate, or concept you are attempting to make habitual in your life. Remember, you can't just break a habit, you won't be successful. You need to replace the old habit with a new one, in order to be successful in the reinvention of you and your life.

Bob Proctor likes to cite the example of a plane flying between New York and Honolulu and how it will deviate from its course at least a hundred times over the course of the flight. The auto pilot (cybernetic mechanism) makes constant corrections to bring it back on course. In other words, you are going to fail your way to your goal. The same goes for your mind. By forming a habit to replace the existing one, you will have created a cybernetic mechanism for your life, this mechanism will keep bringing you back to your goal.

Small trials and tests will present themselves today, and they will continue to present themselves in the future. There will never be a point in time where you can simply release your mind and let it wander. You will never be able to say, "Hey! You know what? I've achieved all I wanted to achieve. I'm done. It's over." As you may already be aware, life is a learning process that never ends. You will continue to learn right up until you draw your last breath.

But don't feel you have to do everything all by yourself. There will be times where you feel as though you could use some help as you trek along the road less traveled. If you feel that way, you are actually in good company. In fact, nearly all truly successful people throughout recorded history have had a coach or a mentor. Having a well of support to draw from is a very effective way to stay motivated, as you venture down the road less traveled.

I've had the privilege of working closely with Presidents, CEO's, Vice Presidents and entire executive teams of some of the largest companies in the world. I've also worked with some of the smallest. I've worked with individual adults and even with children. The common thread among all our clients and students is that they are people who realize they want to succeed at something in life, and it doesn't matter what it is. They recognize that it's okay to ask for help. Not only is it okay, it's a sign of commitment toward achieving your goals.

Here's an interesting question: Where would most people be today if, when they were in their teens, they had the information that is contained in this book? I certainly wish I had it when I was that age.

Now, don't get me wrong, I don't regret what I've done in my life, and I've learned a great deal from some of the decisions that I have made. Use the tools that we've discussed and share them, just as I'm sharing them with you. You will be helping someone else, and it will do wonders for your life as well.

I believe that there would be a substantially greater number of happy people on the planet, if they actually could have incorporated these principles at a young age. It's not just my words that will help pave the way. There's a vast pool of coaches and mentors out there. Bob Proctor, John Assaref, Nido Qubein and many others are teaching people the myriad of ways in which they can achieve all they desire in life. What a different place this world might be today, if we all had understood these principles early on. Thankfully, it's never too early or too late to start.

When I'm speaking at seminars, there is a question that often comes up in various forms: Is my future predetermined? Am I destined to be, or become, something over which I have little or no control? The answer is no. You can achieve anything you want in your life.

The answer to that question then presents two other questions that I like to submit back to you: Are you satisfied with where you are today? If not, what is it you truly want in your life? It's been said that you are exactly where you want to be in your life, if you didn't want to be there, you would do something about it. You would change it for the better.

Remember, when you are contemplating the answer, you must be specific. You can't get away with just saying, "I want to be wealthy." That is too generic. What does wealth mean for you...specifically? What do you want to do with your wealth? If you can answer that question, you will know just how much money you need. You must not only define exactly what you want, but you must also define exactly when you want to achieve it. This applies to all goals, financial or otherwise. Regardless of what you want, it's absolutely imperative that you set a goal!

If you already have a clearly defined goal or picture of what it is you want, then you may be one step ahead of everyone else. Your goals may range from a new home to great health, but your potential is truly unlimited. So dream big. It's likely that you want to improve your position in life. It's just a question of how you want to go about doing it. As each person is unique, the answer may take you down the road less traveled, as it does for many people. Don't let that stop you from pursuing your dreams. When all is said and done in life, you don't regret the things you do, you regret the things you don't do.

Think about it. How many times have you come up with an idea to do something and passed up the opportunity only to be left with an empty feeling of regret upon looking back. On the other hand, if you were ever on the fence about taking a bold step, I'm 100% certain that you will feel great about having taken it. Even if it didn't work out quite the way you had hoped, there is always something that you've gained by getting off the sidelines and getting your uniform dirty. So if the answer to what you want out of life looks like it will be taking you down the road less traveled, you will never regret your decision to pursue it.

CHAPTER 9
YOUR ROAD, WITHOUT FOOTPRINTS

If you want to succeed you should strike out on new paths, rather than travel the worn paths of accepted success.
John D. Rockefeller

• Too many people wait to get confirmation on the relevance of their ideas, before daring to act on them.

• One of the biggest killers of creativity, is conformity.

• Don't let detractors prevent you from going down the road less traveled.

• Just as you were not meant to live in poverty, you were not meant to live a life without challenges.

• Meet every day and every challenge with the idea that you are good enough and you will overcome.

• Life is about service and through service we lift one another higher.

CHAPTER 10

YOUR ACTIONS AND DESERVING SUCCESS

What is not started today is never finished tomorrow.
Johann Wolfgang von Goethe

We've covered a fair bit of ground up to this point. We've talked about the importance of breaking from the past and we've talked about the importance of creating your own economy. We've unveiled the key behind getting all that you want out of life: if you change your mind, you will change your results. We've outlined the ways in which you go about getting what you want by exploring the power of the mind, and showing you just how to use it. We've revealed the fact that you must wholeheartedly believe in your unlimited capabilities to achieve anything that you want in life and that you must first answer one fundamental question: What do you really want?

You may have read this entire book, and though I've asked this question numerous times, have you really thought about the answer?

As you go out in pursuit of your dream, no matter what it is that you decide to do with your life, you need to constantly remind yourself of one irrefutable fact in relation to leading a fulfilling life: you deserve it. You deserve the very best and you owe it to yourself to follow through in fulfilling your desires. We were all given a set of unique gifts. We've all been given special talents and we deserve the rewards that come as a result of us sharing them with the rest of the world.

There's not a shred of doubt in my mind: it was always intended that you live a prosperous and abundant life. Whether this truth comes from God, the universe, energy, or whatever you choose to call it, the fact remains that you were meant to live the life that you've always wanted. I am 100% certain that you were never destined to a life of mediocrity, unhappiness and unfulfilled dreams.

The cure goes back to one central idea that can be found in the title of this book: Change Your Mind, Change Your Results. If you change your mindset, you will cease to lead a dull boring existence, and you will have changed the entire cycle that you have been experiencing, you will have created a new future that will be a shining example to all that are witness to it.

You are now equipped with the necessary knowledge to make a change, the ball is in your court. It's up to you to figure out where you would like to direct your time and your talents. It's up to you to invoke the natural laws of the universe—specifically, the Laws of Attraction, Gestation and ACTION—now go out and fulfill your dreams. If you set the right goals, make an irrevocable decision, and follow the remaining steps as they are laid out in this book, within a short amount of time, you will move in the direction of your goal, and you will reach the destination of your choosing.

You are the only one who can make it happen. You are the one that has to step up, undo that seatbelt, get up off that sofa and take control of and responsibility for your life. Don't make excuses, don't blame anyone or anything, don't make any more plans, don't deliberate any longer... START right now, GO make it HAPPEN! You are the one that has to remain focused on your goals. You are the one that must ensure that your psycho-cybernetic mechanism is engaged, as it will keep you on course, and when the timing is right, bring your thoughts into physical form.

Again, it was always intended that you live an abundant and prosperous life and if you aren't right now, it's not because you can't. It is perhaps because you haven't known how, and now that you have the knowledge and awareness, it is time to choose. Will you ignore this advice and continue on? Or will you choose to empower yourself and achieve more? Write this down, read it, memorize it, and repeat it several times each day: *It was always intended that I have everything that I want and need. It was always intended that I live the life that I desire. I deserve the very best that life has to offer.*

A few chapters back we talked about the six intellectual faculties that all of us possess as human beings. They are all equally important while at the same time, they all have a unique role. I want to revisit one of them as it relates to discovering what you want, that faculty is intuition. Intuition will be a major factor in assisting you in the discovery of the where (the direction) you want to go in life, both now and in the future, and as you hone this faculty you will come to rely on it more and more. There is a very powerful force behind intuition that will guide you along through the path of life. Remember this quote from Dr. Wayne Dyer: "If prayer is you talking to God, then intuition is God talking to you." So what is your intuition telling you? Is it true love that you desire? Is it great health? Great wealth? Whatever it may be, it is imperative that you listen to your intuition, as it will assist you in discovering your true path.

Many of us may say or hear the words, I want a new car or home, but we don't really think about their impact. We don't think about what is really behind the desire that may continuously rise to the surface. You need to consider what may lie beneath. *What is it that you really want?* It's a simple question, but you can't create emotionally engaging goals by glossing it over. Take the time to discover your deepest desires. In the end, it's an individual discovery and no matter what your objective turns out to be, you were born with the innate ability to achieve it. Not only that, but you deserve to have it—whatever "it" may mean for you.

So decide what you want and focus on it to the exclusion of all outside distractions. When you're focused on what you want (and not on what you don't want) resources and solutions will appear. Things will fall into place and though it may seem like coincidence at the time, make no mistake - you have prepared yourself to receive the opportunity. The laws of the universe will work for and with you, whether you are aware of them or not. If you are aware of them, you will be able to utilize their effectiveness to achieve the positive results that you desire.

I was speaking with two of my clients the other day. They are a husband and wife team that I've recently started to work with. The wife pulled me aside to give me their initial payment for my services and she said, "Oh, my husband, he's behaving so negatively about this. He didn't want to part with the money and he's been skeptical about this whole thing." She then went on and on about him in a negative light before assuring me at the end of our conversation that she is actually a very positive person. But is she really?

In my view the husband may not be the issue, perhaps the wife is. She is attracting and enhancing any negative feelings he has and creating a vortex of negativity that is pulling them both down. Release this tendency! Focus on yourself and not on your spouse, your boss or anyone else. Each person must do the work on themselves, and if someone else chooses not to do the work or not to 'get' the concepts, then you can't allow them to hold you back. Never allow your success to be dependent on the actions of another individual.

If you are truly in a positive state, if you are truly living life on a positive plane, then you in most cases won't even notice behaviors that are inconsistent with how you live your life. You will just blow right by them.

As soon as you start talking negatively about someone else, you are putting yourself in a negative state of mind. So, what do you think that you are going to attract in your life as a result? That's right. You are going to attract more of the same. So, unless you switch to a positive thought process, a positive state of mind, you will simply attract more of the things that have been causing your ongoing and undesired state of unhappiness.

In the runaway hit movie, *The Secret*, that came out in 2006, one of the messages in the movie was that you are always receiving into your life what you are putting out into the universe. So if we are focusing on the negative aspects of what others are saying and doing, then we can naturally only expect to get back negativity in return.

An adult has the ability to accept or reject any thought or idea that comes into their conscious mind. Of course the client in the previous example was allowing things that her spouse had supposedly said, into her conscious mind. As a result, those images were impressed upon her subconscious mind which in turn were manifesting in her life. The result was that she was perceived as negative, bitter, and upset by those around her. Interestingly, at the same time, she turned around to me and said, "I'm positive. I'm where I need to be." What we say and what we think are often different, and just saying it doesn't necessarily make it so. Although what we say does have an impact on us, either positive or negative. This is why we have to become emotionally involved with our goals, because lip service (usually negative) will not get us there.

It doesn't matter if you're a sales person, a school teacher, a doctor, a nurse, a lawyer, or a judge, if you are in a negative state of mind, then you will not be effective in life, nor will you be nearly as successful as you could, or should be.

So always remain focused on the good things in life, on what's right with the world. Change your thoughts from negative to positive and allow that attitude to permeate your entire life. One of the best ways to go about doing this, is to go forward with a sense of appreciation for all that you have been given. Gratitude is one of our greatest gifts. The truth is, whether you chose to believe it or not, the two most powerful sources of energy in the world (and remember everything is energy, including you and I) that are available to us are, Love and Gratitude. These powerful forces have the ability, should you so choose, to negate the effects of negativity on you. Approaching life with a genuine sense of gratitude will undoubtedly create the ideals that will allow you to attain phenomenal growth, and the rewards will be extraordinary. It's your positive thought energy that is necessary to attract everything that you've always wanted. If you are truly grateful for what you have been given, then you have already set foot on the road to living a prosperous and abundant life.

Most of us have a pretty good lifestyle. Most of us live in a nice home. Most of us drive a decent car. Even under stressed economic conditions, most of us are still working and most of us are still eating—sometimes too well. But while everyone has the same unlimited potential, not everyone enjoys the same good fortune at the same time. There is a natural cycle to life, therefore don't panic if you can't see "how" something is going to work out. Notwithstanding our focus, there are going to be learning opportunities that will come our way. Ensure that you learn and take away from these opportunities the lessons that will in the future allow you to avoid the same plateaus. No matter where you find yourself in the natural cycle of life, always be grateful for the remarkable blessings that have been bestowed upon you. Of course, never judge another, if you can, offer to assist those that may have hit a plateau, that may need a little lift and that can benefit from your knowledge and experience.

If you take a look at the things in your life that you have to be thankful for, which include family, friends, and all the opportunities that have come your way throughout the course of your lifetime, then you will realize just how truly blessed and fortunate you really are. Sometimes, by virtue of the fact that we tend to over-dissect or over-analyze the things that may not be quite up to our standards, we end up glossing over the fact that we all have a lot to be thankful for.

So when you get that big idea, stay positive. Move forward appreciating what you have in life, and continue to trust your intuition. Don't over-dissect your ideas because you feel that they are imperfect or that you don't have all the answers. Make the decision to act upon the ideas that have come to you. Ask the right questions in pursuit of your goals, really there is only one critical question that we should be asking ourselves: "Is this idea going to move me in the direction of my goal?" If the answer is yes, act on it!

Don't wait for circumstances to change. There will never be a "perfect" set of conditions under which you will have all the answers to all of your questions. This should not prevent you from taking steps toward your goals. Go as far as you can today. As Earl Nightingale once said, "We can let circumstances rule us or we can take charge and rule our lives from within." Don't wait for something else to happen before you make your move. Don't allow your ultimate outcome to be contingent upon someone else's actions. You can't change the actions or behavior of anyone else. You have taken responsibility for your own results. You are the only one that will ensure that your life is taking shape in the way that you have envisioned it.

Even though there are unlimited opportunities out there in the world that are yours for the taking, it's still up to you to take them. Remember, that's not saying that you necessarily have to work harder in order to achieve them. You can always work smarter and more efficiently. Use all of the intellectual faculties at your disposal to find ways in which you can reach your destination along the shortest path.

In the opening of his wonderful little book, *You*^{2}, Price Pritchett tells the true story of sitting in a hotel room near Toronto. He notices a fly, frantically and unsuccessfully, trying to fly through a window to get outside. The fly tries harder and harder, but to no avail. Meanwhile, on the other side of the room sits an open door.

If the fly would only make a minor adjustment in its strategy, it would find that there is a much easier way to success. The point here is that the way to achieving your goals is not necessarily going to involve increasing your level of effort or 'trying harder.' So use the marvelous mind that you have been given and seek solutions in unexpected places.

It can't be stressed enough that there are certain sacrifices that are involved in pursuing your dreams. You have to make a decision as to what you are willing to give up, in order to attain what it is that you truly want in life. We each live full lives and you can't just squeeze a goal in, you have to work toward it as if your life depends on it – because it does. You will shift your attitude to one of "opportunity rather than difficulty," you will then see road blocks as stepping stones.

Our lives are governed by our attitude which is comprised of three familiar elements, these components are thoughts, feelings and actions. Each impacts the other. As long as you're aware of the relationship these have, you'll be able to re-focus if you find yourself veering off course. We're all certainly prone to going off the rails once in a while. As long as you've created your new empowering habits, you'll be able to catch yourself when you feel yourself going astray. You'll be able to refocus your thinking which will redirect your actions, augmenting your results. The cybernetic mechanism that you have established, will bring you back on target and keep you on the right path to your goals.

Don't feel as though you have to do everything on your own. Successful people of today are consistent with the vast majority of successful people throughout recorded history. They have benefited from having a coach or a mentor. It makes sense that if you want different results, you seek out someone who can help, someone who has been there. A big part of this process is accountability, and a good coach or mentor will hold you accountable.

When you face a coach or mentor, there is no lying to yourself or sliding by. You are held to your own words and what you state you want from life. That professional is for your benefit and that benefit will continue long after that particular coach's efforts are long past. We all need a jump start on the learning curve, and that is exactly what a coach provides, among other things.

The truth is that the vast majority of my clients are extremely successful people. They are successful people seeking to achieve even greater gain, to make a quantum leap. They want that accountability that comes with coaching and mentoring. They want to remain focused and remain on target as they pursue their dreams. They want that proverbial kick in the backside every week or two that helps keep them moving in the direction of their ever expanding goals.

You want to associate with mentors, coaches, and individuals who can get you where you want to go, right? Now about the people that you associate with right now on a daily basis. Are they successful? Are they the type of people that want to exceed the limiting expectations that are placed upon them by society? Are they the type of people that are motivated to achieve more in life? Or are they the type of people that are happy with the status quo? Are they the type of people that are happy to come home at five o'clock in the evening and sit on the couch and watch television until they go to bed? Or are they the type of people that are in the process of delving into something bigger in life?

Is his book, *Think and Grow Rich*, Napoleon Hill made an incredible discovery. He uncovered the fact that there are very few successful people out there that deliberate for long periods of time, before making a decision.

He found that successful people make split-second decisions and rarely, if ever, change their minds. I know a lot of people throughout North America and the world that are extremely successful, and this theory certainly holds true with them. Not just in business, but in all aspects of their lives.

So make a decision today. Find a coach or a mentor. Find someone that is committed to help you achieve what it is you really and truly want in life. Find somebody who has been there. Find someone who's been in the trenches. Find someone who has helped and motivated people to achieve their dreams. I would certainly welcome the opportunity to learn more about your aspirations and talk to you about our programs, how we can help you get what you really want. The important thing is to partner with an expert. There are plenty of great coaches and mentors out there.

I'm passionate about what I do because I truly believe that you have untapped potential, and that you can achieve whatever you truly desire and take action on. I trust that I was able to play a small role in helping you get to where you want to go, and give you that little boost to get started.

We've talked throughout the book about the Law of Attraction. With that in mind, I'd like to leave you with one final thought. It's no accident that you have this book in front of you. It's also no accident that you've taken the time to read it all the way through. This book contains information that you've always been seeking. Remember: "the life that you've been seeking has always been seeking you in return." So again, it's no accident that you are right here, right now. It's no accident that you've reached this point in your life. It's no accident that you've reached this point in the book. It's no accident that you wanted this information and that you've finally found it.

Every individual has immense potential just waiting to be discovered, and the information in this book is your discovery. You were destined to read it, but now it's up to you to act upon the concepts presented. You deserve the very best in life, but remember, success is a conscious minute-by-minute decision. Success is not something that you can decide to strive for once this afternoon, expecting to attain it ten years from now. It doesn't work that way. You must be devoted every day. Zig Ziglar sums it up perfectly in one of his many great quotes. He says, "People often say that motivation doesn't last. Well, neither does bathing—that's why we recommend it daily."

So what's stopping you? Is it your paradigms? Is it the group of habits and the pre-programming that you picked up from your parents, educators, and religious leaders throughout your childhood? You don't get a test run at life; this is the real thing so make it count. There are no second takes, so don't wait another moment. Make a conscious and irrevocable decision today to make a positive difference in your life. Make a decision to implement the principles that have been espoused in this book. Don't let the fear of failure or the opinions of others prevent you from achieving the life that you have always wanted. Remember the question, "What would you do in life if you knew you couldn't fail?" Let the answer catapult you toward the life that you have always dreamed of. It's time to change your mind and change your results. You deserve it!

CHAPTER 10
YOUR ACTIONS AND DESERVING SUCCESS

Do you want to know who you are? Don't ask. Act! Action will delineate and define you.
Thomas Jefferson

• You deserve the very best and you owe it to yourself to follow through in fulfilling your desires.

• What we say and what we think are often different and just saying it doesn't make it so.

• Change your vibration from negative to positive and allow it to permeate your life.

• Gratitude has the power to negate negative thoughts.

• The most successful people seek out coaches and mentors to shorten their learning curve.

• Action is the most important determiner of success.

• Change Your Mind, Change Your Results – You deserve it!